# What About Me?

## The forgotten work and ministry of

# The Holy Spirit

## By Dr. Michael D. McClary

You can also learn more about Pastor Mike McClary's Ministries at:

www.cbb-church.com

# Table of Contents

## Author's Introduction

Why another book on the Holy Ghost?  That is the question I asked myself when God was directing me to write this book.  The n the answer came to me:  One of the biggest problems in the church today is a lack of understanding of the work and ministry of the Holy Ghost.  Some people have given credit to the Holy Ghost that should be called the work of the unholy ghost.  It is not the work of God.

Some people, because of fear, have forgotten about His ministry in their personal life as well as His work in the local church.  They miss the power of God.  This is the work of the devil and must be addressed before we can become the force that God would have us to be.

One of the most important things in my life was when I got hold of the Holy Ghost; or should I say, when the Holy Ghost got hold of me.  I hope you will read this book with much prayer, an open mind, an open KJV Bible, and a willingness to find truth.

*Chapter 1*

# The Holy Ghost, His Activities

### His Activities in Creation

The only place to begin to understand the Holy Ghost is to go to the beginning. *In the beginning God created the heaven and the earth. And the earth was without form, and void; and darkness was upon the face of the deep. And the spirit of God moved upon the face of the waters.* (Genesis 1:1-2) *And God said, let us make man in our image, after our likeness: and let them have dominion over the fish of the sea, and over the fowl of the air, and over the cattle, and over all the earth, and over every creeping thing that creepeth upon the earth.* (Genesis 1:26)

The two key words are "spirit" and "us." This is the first mention in the Bible of the Trinity. To understand the Holy Ghost, we must first recognize Him as God. In I John 5:7 we have these words: *For there are three that bear record in heaven, the Father, the Word, and the Holy Ghost: and these three are one.* If you have one of those nearly inspired versions, it says the three are "as one." Throw that thing out and get a real Bible. The Holy Ghost is God and was active in creation. We must understand that the Holy Ghost is God, just as we can say that the Father is God and that Jesus is God, and equal with God.

Yes, the Trinity is one of the mysteries we will never understand until we leave this world – three but one.

Is that not also true of man?  God made man, and man has a spirit, a soul, and a body:  *And the very God of peace sanctify you wholly; and I pray God your whole spirit and soul and body be preserved blameless unto the coming of our lord Jesus Christ.*  (I Thessalonians 5:23)  Some of us are a father, a son, and a husband at the same time.  The important thing here is to see the Holy Ghost as God and active in creation.

## His Activities in the Old Testament

Joseph was equipped by the Holy Ghost to be the prime minister of Egypt (Genesis 41:16,33,37-41).  *[16]And Joseph answered Pharaoh, saying, It is not in me:  God shall give Pharaoh an answer of peace.  [33]Now therefore let Pharaoh look out a man discreet and wise, and set him over the land of Egypt.  [37]And the thing was good in the eyes of Pharaoh, and in the eyes of all his servants.  [38]And Pharaoh said unto his servants, Can we find such a one as this is, a man in whom the Spirit of God is?  [39]And Pharaoh said unto Joseph, Forasmuch as God hath shewed thee all this, there is none so discreet and wise as thou art:  [40]Thou shalt be over my house, and according unto thy word shall all my people be ruled:  only in the throne will I be greater than thou.  [41]And Pharaoh said unto Joseph, See, I have set thee over all the land of Egypt.*

God gave the Spirit to the seventy elders who were to assist Moses as judges.  (Numbers 11:16,17,25)  *[16]And the LORD said unto Moses, Gather unto me seventy men of the elders of Israel, whom thou knowest to be the elders of the people, and officers over them; and bring them unto the tabernacle of the congregation, that they may stand there with thee.* <sup>17</sup>*And I will come down and talk with thee there: and I will take of the spirit which is upon thee, and will put it upon them; and they shall bear the burden of the people with thee, that thou bear it not thyself alone.* <sup>25</sup>*And the LORD came down in a cloud, and spake unto him, and took of the spirit that was upon him, and gave it unto the seventy elders: and it came to pass, that, when the spirit rested upon them, they prophesied, and did not cease.*

The Spirit equipped Joshua to be the successor of Moses: *And the Lord said unto Moses, Take thee Joshua the son of Num, a man in whom is the spirit, and lay thine hand upon him; And set him before Eleazar the priest, and before all the congregation; and give him a charge in their sight.* (Numbers 27:18-19)

The judges were empowered to deliver Israel from their enemies by the power of the Holy Spirit:

*The Spirit came upon Othniel: And the spirit of the Lord came upon him, and he judged Israel, and went out to war: and the Lord delivered Chushan-rishathaim king of Mesopotamia into his hand; and his hand prevailed against Chushan-rishathaim* (Judges 3:10)

*The Spirit came upon Gideon: But the spirit of the Lord came upon Gideon, and he blew a trumpet; and Abiezer was gathered after him.* (Judges 6:34)

*The Spirit came upon Jephthah: Then the spirit of the Lord came upon Jephthah, and he passed over Gilead, and Manasseh, and passed over Mizpeh of Gilead, and from*

*Mizpeh of Gilead he passed over unto the children of Ammon.* (Judges 11:29)

The Holy Spirit came upon the kings of Israel:

*The Spirit came upon Saul*: *And the spirit of God came upon Saul when he heard those tidings, And his anger was kindled greatly.* (I Samuel 11:6) Time and time again we see in the Old Testament that the Spirit of God came upon the man of God, but did not stay as with the New Testament believers. *But the spirit of the Lord departed from Saul, and an evil spirit from the Lord troubled him.* (I Samuel 16:14)

*The Spirit came upon David*: *Then Samuel took the horn of oil, and anointed him in the midst of brethren: and the spirit of the Lord came upon David from that day forward. So Samuel rose up, and went to Ramah*. (I Samuel 16:13) David had seen the Spirit of the Lord depart from Saul, and that was a fear that David had: *Create in me a clean heart, O God; and renew a right spirit within me. Cast me not away from thy presence; and take not thy holy spirit from me. Restore unto me the joy of thy salvation; and uphold me with thy free spirit.* (Psalm 51:10-12)

We can see by the words of Jesus Himself that the Holy Spirit was not dwelling permanently in people until Jesus' ascension. When Jesus' work in salvation was finished, He ascended to heaven and sent the Holy Ghost to indwell the believers: *It is not for you to know the times or the seasons, which the Father hath put in his own power. But ye shall receive power after the Holy Ghost is come upon you: and ye shall be witnesses unto me both in Jerusalem, and in all Judaea, and in Samaria, and unto the uttermost part of the earth.* (Acts 1:7-8)

### His Activities in the Church

His primary work is in salvation:  *And when he is come, he will reprove the world of sin, and of righteousness, and of judgment:  Of sin, because they believe not on me; Of righteousness, because I got to my Father, and ye see me no more; Of judgment, because the prince of this world is judged.*  (John 16:8-11)

The Holy Ghost convicts sinners:  *How then shall they call on him in whom they have not believed?  and how shall they believe in him of whom they have not heard?  and how shall they hear without a preacher?  And how shall they preach, except they be sent?  as it is written, How beautiful are the feet of them that preach the gospel of peace, and bring glad tidings of good things!  But they have not all obeyed the gospel.  For Esaias saith, Lord, who hath believed our report?  So then faith cometh by hearing, and hearing by the Word of God.* (Romans 10:14-17)  *For the preaching of the cross is to them that perish foolishness; but unto us which are saved it is the power of God.*  (I Corinthians 1:18)

The Holy Ghost convicts the unbelievers through the preaching of the Word.  In the Old Testament, the Holy Spirit moved among the prophets and inspired them to be God's spokesmen.  Now in John 1:1 we read, *In the beginning was the Word, and the Word was with God, and the Word was God.*

You see, the Holy Ghost is the key to inspiration and the preserver of the Word of God, and Christ is the Word.

*And he was clothed with a vesture dipped in blood: and his name is called the Word of God.* (Revelation 19:13) You see, the Holy Ghost is not only the preserving factor in the Word of God, but also in the life of the believer. *Jude the servant of Jesus Christ, and brother of James, to them that are sanctified by God the Father, and preserved in Jesus Christ, and called:* (Jude 1:1) *And grieve not the holy spirit of God, whereby ye are sealed unto the day of redemption.* (Ephesians 4:30)

Do you see why the devil is doing all he can to water down the Bible? It is the living Word; there is no life outside of Christ (the Word).

The Holy Ghost convicts unbelievers that they are sinners because they do not believe in Jesus Christ as Lord and Savior. The sin of unbelief is the basic root of all sin. To reject Jesus Christ as God's Son and as man's Savior is the sin that condemns people to exclusion from the Kingdom of God. We will talk more on the subject of sinning away your day of grace. *And when He is come, He will reprove the world of sin, and of righteousness, and of judgment: of sin because they believe not on me...* (John 16:8-9)

The following was taken from the footnotes of the Liberty Annotated Study Bible King James Version: "The word 'conviction' embraces a number of biblical expressions in its meaning. Originally it derived from two Latin terms meaning 'cause to see'. The New Testament uses the terms 'reproof', 'conviction', and 'illumination' to communicate the ministry of the Holy Spirit where-by He causes the individual to 'see' (understand) the truth."

The Holy Ghost convicts unbelievers in regard to righteousness. He uses the gospel message of the death, resurrection, and ascension of Jesus Christ to reveal that God vindicated Jesus Christ and exalted Him as the One who was altogether righteous. *Of righteousness, because I go to my Father, and ye see me no more*. (John 16:10) This was God's manner of placing His stamp of approval on the redemptive acts of Jesus Christ. The death of Christ for our sins reveals the sinfulness of our transgressions and our need for the perfect righteousness of Jesus Christ that comes through faith. *For I delivered unto you first of all that which I also received how that Christ died for our sins according to the scriptures; And that he was buried, and that he rose again the third day according to the scriptures*. (I Corinthians 15:3-4)

There are four vital truths here, introduced by:

"That Christ died for our sins." This is a substitutionary and propitiatory sacrifice. *Even the righteousness of God which is by faith of Jesus Christ unto all and upon all them that believe: for there is no difference: For all have sinned, and come short of the glory of God; Being justified freely by his grace through the redemption that is in Christ Jesus: whom God hath set forth to be a propitiation through faith in His blood, to declare his righteousness for the remission of sins that are past, through the forbearance of God; To declare, I say, at this time his righteousness: that he might be just, and the justifier of him which believeth in Jesus.* (Romans 3:22-26)

"That He was buried" - This evidences the reality and totality of His death.

"That He rose again" - The perfect tense stresses abiding results--- He was raised in the past and remains alive now.

"According to the scriptures" – The facts of the gospel are not only important historically, but prophetically as well. They occurred as had been predicted.

The Holy Ghost convicts unbelievers in regard to judgment. *Of judgment because the prince of this world is judged.* (John 16:11) Satan thought that he had accomplished a great victory by instigating the crucifixion of Jesus Christ. Seemingly, Christ in the tomb was a victim. But God raised Christ back to life and thus repudiated the accomplishments of the satanic forces. What seemed to be a satanic victory was revealed to be a satanic defeat. The devil is a defeated foe, and all who follow him will be losers. Let's look at John 16:11 again: *Of judgment because the prince of this world is judged.* The power of Christ to judge satan and to overthrow his kingdom is not future, but at the cross and the resurrection. "Is judged" (kekritai) means "has been judged."

It is not the task of a pastor, a Sunday school teacher, a parent, or anyone else to convict the unbeliever that he or she is a sinner in need of God's forgiveness and the gift of new life. Only the Holy Spirit can do this.

## Chapter One Review

1. The _____ _____ is God and was _____ in creation.

2. The Holy Spirit was not _____ in people until Jesus' _____.

3. In the Old Testament, the Holy Spirit _____ among the Prophets and _____ them to be God's _____.

4. The Holy Ghost is the key to _____ and the _____ of the Word of God. _____ is the Word.

5. The sin of _____ is the basic _____ of all sin.

6. The four vital truths are:

    a)_____

    b)_____

    c)_____

    d)_____

7. The Holy Ghost:

    a) Convicts unbelievers _____

    b) Convicts unbelievers _____

    c) Convicts unbelievers _____

    d) Convicts unbelievers_____

*Chapter 2*

# The Holy Ghost, The Comforter

### The Comforter for Isolation

*If ye love me, keep my commandments. And I will pray the Father, and he shall give you another Comforter, that he may abide with you for ever; Even the spirit of truth; whom the world cannot receive, because it seeth him not, neither knoweth him: but ye know him; for he dwelleth with you, and shall be in you. I will not leave you comfortless: I will come to you. Yet a little while, and the world seeth me no more; but ye see me: because I live, ye shall live also. At that day ye shall know that I am in my Father, and ye in me, and I in you. He that hath my commandments, and keepeth them, he it is that loveth me: and he that loveth me shall be loved of my Father, and I will love him, and will manifest myself to him.* (John 14:15-21)

There are many Christians, but we are always in a minority in this world. The world may respect us as persons, but they resent us as Christians. We can expect to be shunned and even shamed in this world, just like Jesus was. What a blessing we see in this chapter, that Jesus' first request to the Father was to send another comforter. "Another" stresses that the Holy Spirit would be "another" like Jesus. A comforter is an advocate called alongside for aid in times of trouble. The Greek word "parakletos" literally means, "one called alongside to help." The word "parakletos" is found five times in the Bible. Four times it is translated "comforter" (John 14:16, John 14:26, John 15:26, John 16:7), and one time it is translated "advocate." (I John 2:1) According to Vine, it suggests the capability or adaptability to give aid. It was used in a court of justice to denote a legal assistant, counsel for the defense, an advocate. In general, it was one who pleads another's cause; an intercessor or advocate like Jesus is for us. In the widest sense, it signifies a comforter. Christ was this to His disciples by the implication of His word when He said He would send them "another comforter." Jesus Christ is truly "the consolation of Israel" and the Christian's advocate. By way of His Holy Spirit, He still is a present help in time of need.

Let's look at how the problem of isolation is taken care of by the comforter:

A Premise: *If ye love me, keep my commandments.* (John 14:15) Jesus, having assured His disciples that He was not deserting them but rather going before to prepare a place for them, proceeded to ask for their obedience. *If ye love me, keep my commandments.* Let me give you food for thought: if their distress over the prediction of His departure was genuine, it meant that they loved Him. If they really loved Him, they must show it by obedience. Dear reader, love must be the motive in our lives; obedience to Him must be the standard for our activity. We can never expect comfort apart from obedience; there is no comfort in disobedience. My friend, there is only doubt and discomfort.

Devotion to Christ is reasonable. Are we not endeared to people who do much less for us that Christ did for us?

How much more should we love the Redeemer when we remember what He is and what He has done! *Greater love hath no man than this, that a man lay down his life for his friends. Ye are my friends if ye do whatsoever I command you.* (John 15:13-14)

<u>Duty to Christ will be the result</u>. *Verily, verily I say unto you, He that believeth on me, the works that I do shall he do also; and greater works than these shall he do; because I go unto my Father.* (John 14:12) Let me say that the thought of love follows that of faith. Faith issues in works of power; love, in works of devotion. This is what James spoke about: *Yea, a man may say, thou hast faith, and I have works: show me thy faith without thy works and I will show thee my faith by my works.* (James 2:18)

Obedience is the necessary consequence of love. Love carries with it practical devotion, and this calls out the intercession of the Lord; or, in other words, love for Christ finds practical expression in love for the brethren, which is Jesus' commandment: *A new commandment I give unto you, that ye love one another; as I have loved you, that ye also love one another.* (John 13:34)

<u>A Promise</u>: *And I will pray the Father, and he shall give you another Comforter, that he may abide with you forever; Even the Spirit of truth; whom the world cannot receive, because it seeth him not, neither knoweth him: but ye know him; for he dwelleth with you, and shall be in you.* (John 14:16-17) Have you ever asked yourself, "Why didn't Jesus remain on earth after the conflict was past and victory was won?" *O death, where is thy sting? O grave, where is thy victory? The sting of death is sin; and the strength of sin*

is the law.  *But thanks be to God, which giveth us the victory through our Lord Jesus Christ.*  (I Corinthians 15:55-57)  Why not, after the resurrection, take His great power and reign as a conqueror over sin and death; rule with good influence over our fallen race until all the earth acknowledged His power?

We don't know all the reasons, and I'm sure God is not interested in our opinions, but, couldn't one reason be that God compels no man to believe by external force?  *For God so loved the world, that he gave his only begotten son, that whosoever believeth in him should not perish, but have everlasting life.*  (John 3:16)  The kingly glory of Jesus on earth would have been such a force that there would be no room left for faith, or even for free choice, on the part of men.  We must also remember the sovereignty of God, who does things on His timetable.

Remember that salvation is not a state that can be produced by external force---human nature is not like some plastic substance that can be molded by external pressure.  Salvation is brought about, not against, but with the sinner's will.  The guilt of sin is removed by Christ's death; but the power of sin is subdued by spiritual and moral influences appealing to mind and heart.  This is the way that the Holy Ghost works within man, touching the inner being by His gracious influences, penetrating it with subtle unseen power, quickening the new spiritual life, strengthening, comforting, and guiding.  Jesus had been the "comforter" of disciples; but now that He must depart, He gives this blessed promise of another paraclete who would dwell with them forever.

**Let's look at the description of this promised one:**

He is an answer to Jesus' prayer to the Father: *And I will pray the Father, and he shall give you another comforter, that he may abide with you for ever.* (John 14:16)

He is another "comforter": *He shall give you another.* (v 16)

He dwells permanently with the believer: *That he may abide with you for ever.* (v 16)

He is the Spirit of Truth: *Even the spirit of truth.* (John 14:17)

He is unknown to the "world:" *Whom the world cannot receive, because it seeth him not, neither knoweth him.* (v 17)

He will dwell in the believer: *For he dwellth with you, and shall be in you.* (v 17)

A Presence: *I will not leave you comfortless: I will come to you. Yet a little while, and the world seeth me no more; but ye see me: because I live, ye shall live also. At that day ye shall know that I am in my Father, and ye in me, and I in you. He that hath my commandments, and keepeth them, he it is that loveth me: and he that loveth me shall be loved of my Father, and I will love him, and will manifest myself to him.* (John 14:18-21)

The statement *I will not leave you comfortless* has the meaning "I will not leave you orphans." Think for a moment on the experience of the disciples as Jesus spoke of His speedy departure. It must have been that of a child standing at the bedside of a dying parent. Christ had been everything to them during the past three years. They had learned to look to Him, lean on Him, and follow Him! He had asked them to forsake all and follow Him. *So likewise, whosoever he be of you that forsaketh not all that he hath, he cannot be my disciple.* (Luke 14:33) The word "forsaketh" means literally "renounce" or "give up." How they enjoyed their relationship! Each day they drew closer to Him; each new day some further revelation of Christ's power, wisdom, or love had dawned upon them, until He had become all-in-all to them. And now the end was drawing near, as He told them. Yet a brief space and they would be left alone, orphaned spiritual children in an unsympathetic and hostile world. But to their troubled minds came these words of comfort and promise: *I will not leave you comfortless (orphans).* (John 14:18)

The disciples were not orphans, for they could rejoice in the Heavenly Father's care. If a person is fatherless, he is deprived of a father's love and care. My father died when I was only a year old, and I was passed from one home to another. At the age of seven I moved in with my grandmother, who was raising my brother and sister. She loved me, but I was deprived of a father's love. I lived a life looking to fill an empty spot in my life. I found Jesus as my personal Savior, and then I found the love of a father, of which I had been deprived. But the disciples lacked nothing. Jesus had spoken to them and filled their hearts with assurance of the Father's love and care, in which they could rejoice.

They were not orphans, because Christ Himself would come to them. *The Lord is risen indeed, and hath appeared to Simon.* (Luke 24:34) They would see Him in His resurrection glory, so then they could greet one another with words like "The Lord is risen." Their lives were bound up with His life so that His life was now their life. His presence was no imagination, no dream, but a great spiritual reality.

They were not orphans, for they would be indwelt by the Holy Ghost. Tenney said that the Holy Spirit is the token difference between the Christian and the unbeliever. "The world" cannot receive Him. He indwells the Christian. As Paul said, *Now if any man have not the Spirit of Christ, he is none of his.* (Romans 8:9) Yes, my friend, the measure of the fullness of the Spirit may vary in the individual life, but the presence of the Spirit is essential to true Christian experiences. Let us remember that the difference between "with you" and "in you" (v 17) is significant, for it shows that, whereas the Spirit was watching over the disciples at the time when Jesus spoke, a crisis was coming in which the Spirit would enter into the lives of the disciples and control them from within. He is our Comforter for isolation.

## The Comforter For Ignorance

*These things have I spoken unto you, being yet present with you. But the Comforter, which is the Holy Ghost, whom the Father will send in my name, he shall teach you all things, and bring all things to your remembrance, whatsoever I have said unto you. Peace I leave with you, my peace I give unto you: not as the world giveth, give I unto you. Let not your heart be troubled, neither let it be afraid.* (John 14:25-27)

I read an introduction in the "Minister's Manna," dated October 11, 1998, that really jumped out at me: "A brisk little lady inquired at a travel agency about a certain European tour. The agent mentioned that this particular tour included the Passion Play at Oberammergau. The woman drew herself up to her full five-feet-one-inches and replied icily, "I'm sick and tired of all this sex stuff---and I'm surprised at you!" Then she stormed out. When I read that, it reminded me of all the ignorance around today. There seems to be so much we don't know about today that it sometimes gets discouraging. It's like one fellow said, "The more I study, the more I know; the more I know, the more I forget; the more I forget, the less I know; so why study?"

We must admit there is much about the Bible that we don't know; even some of the things that we do know about we don't understand. Do you ever find yourself getting discouraged? We need comfort for our ignorance. And this is where the Comforter comes in. Our Comforter is not only a comfort for our isolation, but also for ignorance. Only the Lord knows how ignorant we are at times about spiritual things. We need His help. That is one reason the Lord left the Holy Spirit with us to indwell us.

Please, remember the word "parakletos" is found five times in the Greek. Four times it is translated "comforter" (John 14:16, John 15:26, John 16:7) and one time it is translated "advocate." (I John 2:1) Don't forget it means called to one's side, that is, to one's aid.

Yes, we certainly have difficulty with spiritual ignorance at times. And if you're like me, it is very disheartening to be ignorant and know it. I remember that day I came to know Christ as my personal Savior; I could read at only about a third grade level, yet I was trying to understand God's word. The I found, *But the comforter, which is the Holy Ghost, whom the Father will send in my name, He shall teach you all things, and bring all things to your remembrance, whatsoever I have said unto you.* (John 14:26) My friend, always ask the Holy Ghost to reveal truth to you. Never read God's Word without the Holy Ghost's revealing power. Remember, the Holy Ghost is the Revealer; Jesus is the Revelation. Notice how the Holy Spirit, our Comforter helps:

He Is The Teacher Of The Faithful (John 14:25-26)

Jesus had to depart, but He promised to send His Spirit in place of His own immediate presence. "I will not leave you comfortless." The "Paraclete," which is the Holy Ghost, shall come and lead you to higher attainments than those you have yet reached. He shall not only call to remembrance all things which have been spoken unto you, but shall teach you all things, and lead you to understand what has been revealed.

The Holy Ghost is the divine Teacher of the Church. For three years the disciples had been in the company of Christ. They had been learning of Him *In whom are hid all the treasures of wisdom and knowledge.* (Colossians 2:3) Yes, they had received a training, such as no university can ever give. Like some of us, it seems as though they didn't make a very good grade. After His resurrection, the Lord spoke of some of them as *fools, and slow of heart to believe all that the prophets had spoken.* (Luke 24:25) Even on the eve of His ascension, they were far from understanding His teaching. *When they therefore were come together, they asked of him, saying, Lord, wilt thou at this time restore again the Kingdom to Israel? And he said unto them, It is not for you to know the times or the seasons, which the Father hath put in his own power. But ye shall receive power after that the Holy Ghost is come upon you: and ye shall be witnesses unto me both in Jerusalem, and in all Judea, and in Samaria, and unto the uttermost part of the earth.* (Acts 1:6-8)

But look at them after Pentecost. A mighty change has taken place in them. A flood of light seems to have been poured on the teaching of Jesus. What was dark and mysterious before, was now bright as the morning sun. Don't miss the lesson about reading and studying the Scriptures. Who says we must understand everything when we read the Bible? It may not be until later, as we let the Spirit teach, that we understand a spiritual truth. Just keep praying to the Holy Ghost to reveal truth. Keep reading, keep studying, keep meditating on His Word, and let the Holy Ghost do His job of enlightenment as He wills.

He Is Teacher Of The Faith. (v.26)

The disciples had not fully understood all of Christ's teachings. Sometimes it seemed to them that He spoke in riddles. But after the resurrection and the descent of the Spirit, what appeared to be dark and obscure became light: *And as I began to speak, the Holy Ghost fell on them, as on us at the beginning. Then remembered I the word of the Lord, how that he said, "John indeed baptized with water; but ye shall be baptized with the Holy Ghost."* (Acts 11:15-16) As the Reverend W. Frank Scott said, "The heavenly

Sower had scattered the seeds of divine truth into hearts prepared to receive it; but there was needed the outpouring of the Spirit, with heavenly influence, the dews and rains of grace, to awaken it to life, to cause it to spring forth and bloom into fuller fruitfulness."

Let me say something that is very important about truth: We are not told anywhere that the Holy Ghost was to teach the apostles any *new* truth. There are some today who give the Holy Ghost a ministry of teaching new truth. My friend, always put your trust in the Word of God. The Holy Ghost is to *teach you all things, and bring all things to your remembrance, whatsoever I have said unto you.* (John 14:26B) You see, He is to instruct in, and call to remembrance what the Master, Himself, had already taught. The Spirit has everything necessary to do the job; and we, as believers, have the Spirit.

He has the AUTHORITY. *Whom the Father will send in my name* conveys the concept of authority in revelation. Please make a note of the following: *In my name* appears thirteen times in the Gospel of John. How many? Six of these instances refer to prayer *in the name* of Jesus. Almost all mean that one person acts on the authority of another, as supported by the personality behind the name. Jesus illustrates this point when He said, *I am come in my Father's name, and ye receive me not: if another shall come in his own name, him ye will receive.* (John 5:43) The Holy Ghost, sent in Jesus' name, would come with His authority, and the message of the Spirit should be received as if Jesus Himself were speaking.

He has the ANSWERS. *He shall teach you all things* shows that the Holy Ghost will be the believer's tutor. His instruction assures the clarity of revelation. We need to remember that many of Christ's teaching were obscure to His disciples because they did not have the spiritual background to understand His underlying thought. That's why He assured them of *another Comforter.* Jesus did not give them a fixed system of proposition to be memorized in order to ensure their perception of His truth. Instead, He promised them the presence of the active, living Spirit, who could speak of Him with convicting power. I John 2:20 says, *But ye have an unction,* (if I may, an anointer, which allows you to discern between truth and error*) from the Holy One, and ye know all things.* I John 2:27 says, *But the anointing which ye have received of Him abideth in you, and ye need not that any many teach you: but as the same anointing teacheth you of all things, and is truth, and is no lie, and even as it hath taught you, ye shall abide in him.*

This doesn't mean we don't need pastors, teachers, and evangelists*: And he gave some apostles, and some prophets, and some evangelists; and some pastors and teachers; for the perfecting of the saints, for the work of the ministry, for the edifying of the body of Christ.* (Ephesians 4:11-12) It does mean that a string of degrees won't help us understand spiritual things without the Spiritual Teacher, the Holy Ghost.

He has the AWARENESS. *Bring all things to your remembrance* assures the continuity of revelation. All the apostles were to preach, and some of them were to write the things that Jesus did and taught, to translate them to distant nations and future ages. If man had been left to himself, some needful things might have been forgotten, others misrepresented, through the treachery of memories. Therefore, the Spirit is promised to enable them to truly relate and record what Jesus said to them. Let me assure you that *calling to remembrance* implies learning, for men cannot remember what they never knew. *Study to show thyself approved unto God, a workman that needeth not to be ashamed, rightly dividing the word of the truth*. (II Timothy 2:15)  Jesus did not intend that the Holy Ghost should be regarded as a substitute for learning. He expected that the disciples would pay close attention to His teachings, so that the Spirit might direct the knowledge they had acquired for personal and public profit.  Those who would teach the things of God must first, themselves, be taught of God; this is the Spirit's work:  *"As for me, this is my covenant with them, saith the Lord; My spirit that is upon thee, and my words which I have put in thy mouth, shall not depart out of thy mouth, nor out of the mouth of thy seed, nor out of the mouth of thy seed's seed, saith the Lord, from henceforth and forever."*  (Isaiah 59:21)

He Is Teaching Faithfully (v.26)

The *"you"* does not limit the teaching of the Spirit to the apostles who were the representatives of the church.  It is a present reality.  The Holy Ghost continues faithfully to teach all the saints of all ages.


**The Comforter For Inadequacy**

*If the world hate you, ye know that it hated me before it hated you. If ye were of the world, the world would love his own: but because ye are not of the world, but I have chosen you out of the world, therefore the world hateth you. Remember the word that I said unto you, The servant is not greater than his lord. If they have persecuted me, they will also persecute you; if they have kept my saying, they will keep yours also. But all these things will they do unto you for my name's sake, because they know not him that sent me. If I had not come and spoken unto them, they had not had sin: but now they have no cloak for their sin. He that hateth me hateth my Father also. If I had not done among them the works which none other man did, they had not had sin: but now have they both seen and hated both me and my Father. But this cometh to pass, that the word might be fulfilled that is written in their law, They hated me without a cause. But when the Comforter is come, whom I will send unto you from the Father, even the Spirit of truth, which proceedeth from the Father, he shall testify of me: And ye also shall bear witness, because ye have been with me from the beginning.* (John 15:18-27)  In this chapter of John we see a conference on relationships. We see the relationship of the believers to Jesus (vs.1-11), the relationship of believers to each other (vs.12-17), and the relationship of believers to the world (vs.15-27). Please note that in every relationship we seem to be inadequate.

## The Relationship Of Believers To Jesus

We prove inadequate in our relationship with Jesus when we depend on ourselves and live self-centered lives. We need to keep in mind that our main purpose as

Christians is to bear fruit. This purpose will always be inadequate unless we depend on Christ and produce fruit. Take a close look at John 15:5, *I am the vine, ye are the branches: He that abideth in me, and I in him, the same bringeth forth much fruit: for without me ye can do nothing.*

### The Relationship Of Believers To Each Other

We prove inadequate in our relationship with other believers way too often. Just as the disciples were unstable, so are we. The differences of temperament among them and jealousies that had arisen over their positions, we still see today. Jesus knew that if they were to maintain an adequate testimony for Him, they could do so only as a unit. Disunity only hampers the work, and I believe it is slowly killing it. That's why it's important for us to apply verse 12: *This is my commandment, that ye love one another as I have loved you.* Please note the elements in this kind of love:

1.) Sacrifice (v.13)

2.) Intimacy (v.15)

3.) Initiative (v.16)

4.)Productivity (v.16) – a relationship that produces results in its exchange.

Let me meddle a moment. If we would befriend others as Christ befriended the disciples, we could help produce some solid workers for the Lord's vineyard. Not only that, but the only way we will ever have revival in our land is for Christians to humble themselves and face up to the possibility that the other person might be right.

## The Relationship Of Believers To The World

We often prove inadequate in our relationship to the world as well. Our job is to win them to Christ, and we fail miserably. Verse 17 was to be the rule and law for the New Testament believer: *These things I command you, that ye love one another.* Today, most of Christianity wants to be part of the world. We are trying to become *of* this world. I have even heard preachers say that we are to bring in the millennial reign of Christ. You see, they feel so in love with this world that they want Christ to come and set up a kingdom without judgment of this wicked world. They believe that signs and wonders will save everyone. If we look at verse 18, however, we see that a Spirit-filled Christian will have conflict in the world. *If the world hate you, ye know that it hated me before it hated you.* Don't miss this: just as the world hated and persecuted the Master because the truth which He is and which He taught brought condemnation to the world, so would it be with the disciples, then and now. Hatred and persecution, He said, would follow their course through the world.

Again, for a moment, put yourself in the sandals of the disciples. These are not the most encouraging words. You see, now Jesus is telling them how much the world will hate, persecute, and even kill them because of Him, and adds, "By the way, I won't be here when it happens." He surely has a way of making us feel inadequate. My friend, we need comfort for our inadequacy. That is where the Comforter comes in. Our relationship to the world in winning them to Christ will prove useless without Him.

Let's talk for a moment about the world's hostile resistance to that which is spiritual. Jesus never intended for the believer to live in pious isolation. We must live in the world, but we must not be of the world. As Merrill C. Tenney said, "Between the two is a hostility which is as deep and as inevitable as their nature – a hostility which goes back to the enmity of the carnal mind against God." The Bible says, *"Because the carnal mind is enmity against God; for it is not subject to the law of God, neither indeed can be. So then they that are in the flesh cannot please God."* (Romans 8:7-8)

### The source of the world's hatred.

Satan - *"In whom the god of this world hath blinded the minds of them which believe not, lest the light of the glorious gospel of Christ, who is the image of God, should shine unto them."* (II Corinthians 4:4) Those who are a part of this world are not conformed to God. Remember, God is light, the world is darkness; God is love, the world, hatred.

Sin - (Romans 8:7-8) It's that sin nature that is controlling the unregenerate man, and causes enmity to God and causes hatred to His cause.

Religion - *But this cometh to pass, that the word might be fulfilled that is written in their law, They hated me without cause.* (John 15:25) Religion has always hated Christ in the sense that the religious love their works more than God's grace; they love their hypocrisy rather than truth; they accept sin instead of righteousness.

The World And The Spirit

*But when the Comforter is come, who I will send unto you from the Father, even the Spirit of truth, which proceedeth from the Father, he shall testify of me. And ye also shall bear witness because ye have been with me from the beginning.* (John 15:26-27) The Lord has just dwelt on the hatred with which He had been met. Yet, that was not to prevail. He now contrasts the hostility of the world with the power by which it should be overcome. Oh to be *"more than conquerors through him that loved us."* (Romans 8:37)

Merrily C. Tenney said it well: "Jesus expected that the Holy Spirit and the disciples through whom He would work would maintain the words and deeds which he had begun, and through which the evil of the world would meet its living refutation." Thank the Lord the Holy Ghost witnesses first, and then we witness. Yes, He is our comforter for inadequacy. Remember, this is the only way souls can be saved and we can be useful witnesses for Christ.

## The Comforter For Inability

*Nevertheless I tell you the truth; It is expedient for you that I go away: for if I go not away, the Comforter will not come unto you; but if I depart, I will send him unto you. And when he is come, he will reprove the world of sin, and of righteousness, and of judgment: Of sin, because they believe not on me; Of righteousness, because I go to my Father, and ye see me no more; Of judgment, because the prince of this world is judged. I have yet many things to say unto you, but ye cannot bear them now. Howbeit when he, the Spirit of truth, is come, he will guide you into all truth: for he shall not speak of himself; but whatsoever he shall hear, that shall he speak: and he will show you things to come. He shall glorify me: for he shall receive of mine, and shall show it unto you. All things that the Father hath are mine: therefore said I, that he shall take of mine, and shall show it unto you. A little while, and ye shall not see me: and again, a little while, and ye shall see me, because I go to the Father. Then said some of his disciples among themselves, What is this that he saith unto us, 'A little while, and ye shall not see me: and again, a little while, and ye shall see me:' and, 'Because I go to the Father?'* (John 16:7-17)

Having made clear in chapter 15 that the hatred of the world was inevitable for disciples if they would follow Him, Jesus proceeded, in chapter 16, to make even more vivid what that hatred would mean. The obvious and natural reaction of the disciples to Jesus' prediction was depression. (v.6) But to dispel the gloom, He informed them that His departure was not just an inevitable calamity that must be endured, but also a necessity to the progress of the work. It would be profitable for Him to go, because His death would enlarge His ministry through the activity of the Holy Ghost.

As it was usual for the Old Testament prophets to comfort believers in their calamities with the promise of the Messiah: *"For unto us a child is born, unto us a son is given: and the government shall be upon his shoulder; and his name shall be called Wonderful, Counselor, The mighty God, The everlasting Father, The Prince of Peace;"* (Isaiah 9:6) and *"Hear now, O Joshua the high priest, thou, and thy fellows that sit before thee: for they are men wondered at: for,* behold, I will bring forth my servant the BRANCH," (Zechariah 3:8) so Jesus the Messiah had come, and now He comforts the believers with the promise of the Comforter.

Let's review the definition of the word "Comforter." It is "Parakletos," and is found five times in the Bible. Four times it is translated "Comforter," (John 14:16, 14:26, 15:26, 16:7) and one time it is translated "Advocate." (I John 2:1) It means "Called to one's side," that is, to one's aid. It was used in a court of justice to denote a legal assistant, counsel for the defense, an advocate. According to Vine, it suggests the capability or adaptability for giving aid. In general, it is one who pleads another's cause; an intercessor or advocate like Jesus is for us. In the widest sense, it signifies a securer or comforter.

My friend, this is the kind of comfort we need when we realize that the command to the disciples to reach the whole world for Christ is our command as well. The torch has been passed to us. Again, let's just try to imagine how the apostles felt when Jesus told them He was leaving. He told them to *go and bring forth fruit*. He wanted them to go to the whole world with the gospel. That, my friend, is a task! They knew they couldn't get the job done without Jesus. Now it is our job, and as the disciples did not have the ability to get the job done, we need comfort for our inability. That's where the Comforter comes in, and that's why Jesus said the Spirit needed to come.

### The Comforter Comes (John 16:7)

The Savior Must Depart – It was absolutely necessary for Jesus to depart so the Comforter could come. Jesus expressed that fact negatively and positively.

The Spirit Will Descend – *If I depart I will send Him to you.* It's as if Jesus said, "Trust me to provide effectively so you won't be a loser when I depart." Praise the glorified Redeemer; He is not unmindful of His church on earth, nor will He ever leave it without its necessary supports. What a Savior! Though He departs, He sends the Comforter. As a matter of fact, He departs with the purpose of sending the Comforter.

## The Comforter Convicts (John 16:8-11)

His Task To Reprove – The spirit, by the WORD and conscience, is a reprove, and He uses ministers to work through.

His Task To Convince – This is a legal term and speaks of the office of a judge in summing up the evidence and settling a matter that has been long covered over, in clear and true light.

He shall "convince"; that is, He shall put to silence the adversaries of Christ and His cause by discovering and demonstrating the falsehood and fallacy of that which they have opposed. Remember, this is the Spirit's job, not yours or mine. We may open the cause, but only the Holy Ghost can open the heart. We must be faithful to do our part: *"Preach the WORD; be instant in season, out of season; reprove, rebuke, exhort with all longsuffering and doctrine."* (II Timothy 4:2)

His Target – The target is the world, both Jew and Gentile. *"And said unto them, Thus it is written, and thus it behooved Christ to suffer, and to rise from the dead the third day: and that repentance and remission of sins should be preached in His name among all nations, beginning at Jerusalem."* (Luke 24:46,47) The disciples were to go to the whole world with the Gospel, and Jesus said that they would be persecuted for His sake. Do not forget that the same call is ours today. Because of the convincing work of the Holy Ghost, we can be assured that there will be many who will be convicted of their sin and trust the Savior. We just need to keep witnessing, keep going, and keep withstanding as we find those who are convinced of their sin and ready to trust Christ. This is our duty until He returns.

## The Comforter Comforts (John 16:12-15)

The coming of the Holy Ghost was to be a great advantage for the disciples. You see, the Holy Ghost has work to do, not only on the enemies of the Cross, to convince and humble them, but upon us, as well, to instruct and comfort us; therefore, it was expedient for them that Jesus go away.

### He Guides The Saints (vs.12-13)

What a comfort it is to know that we have a guide in this dark and evil world. The Holy Ghost will guide us into the whole truth and nothing but the truth. May I say, and we will cover this more, the Bible is truth, and the Holy Ghost will always work in the realm of the Bible. He can lead us around the pitfalls, and He can go before us and witness to those to whom we witness, even before we get there. We just go and pick ripe fruit.

### He Glorified The Savior (vs.14-15)

What a comfort it is to know that the Holy Ghost is not selfish.  He does not even speak of Himself.  Always remember this – it will help you in discerning the truth:  he always speaks for the Lord and points everyone to Him.  Any movement that points to the Holy Ghost is not of God.  The emphasis must always be on Christ, because our purpose is to win men, women, boys, and girls to Christ.  Sometimes, when we follow men, we see them use us for their own selfish purpose.  Not so with the Comforter.  What a breath of fresh air in a self-centered, self-seeking world.

### Chapter Two Review

1.  The Holy Ghost is the Comforter for:

_____

2.  _____ must be the motive in our lives; _____ must be the standard for our activity.

3.  There is no comfort in: _____

4.  Faith issues in works of _____ while love issues in works _____

5.  List aspects of the Holy Spirit found in John 14:16-17:

a.)_____

b.)_____

c.)_____

d.)_____

e.)_____

f.)_____

6. Christians are not orphans because

a.)_____

b.)_____

c.)_____

7. The Holy Ghost comforts us in our ignorance because He is _____ and _____

8. According to John 14:26, what does the Holy Spirit have that qualifies him to be our teacher?

a.)_____

b.)_____

c.)_____

9. Explain how we are inadequate in each of the following relationships:

a.) The Believer and Jesus

_____

b.) The Believer and Other Believers

_____

c.) The Believer and The World

_____

10. The sources of the world's hatred of believers are:

a.)_____

b.)_____

c.)_____

11. List the jobs believers are unable to do without the Holy Spirit, according to John 16:7-15:

a.)_____

b.)_____

c.)_____

d.)_____

e.)_____

12. What is a breath of fresh air in our self-centered, self-seeking world?

_____

_____

*Chapter 3*

# The Works Of The Holy Spirit

There are seven words used in the New Testament in connection with the ministry of the Holy Spirit in this Church age. Every one of these words has a different meaning. They are never used interchangeably.

1. *Born* of the Spirit (John 3:5)

2. *Indwelt* of the Spirit (II Timothy 1:14; Romans 8:11)

3. *Sealed* by the Spirit (II Corinthians 1:22; Ephesians 4:30)

4. *Anointed* by the Spirit (II Corinthians 1:21; I John 2:27)

5. *Earnest* of the Spirit (II Corinthians 1:22; Ephesians 1:14)

6. *Filled* with the Spirit (Ephesians 5:18)

7. *Baptized* of the Spirit (Matthew 3:11; Acts 1:5; Corinthians 12:13)

In this chapter we will look at the first of these words:

Born of the Spirit (John 3:3-7)

*Jesus answered and said unto him, Verily, verily, I say unto thee, Except a man be born again, he cannot see the kingdom of God. Nicodemus saith unto him, How can a man be born when he is old? Can he enter the second time into his mother's womb, and be born?          Jesus answered, Verily, verily, I say until thee, Except a man be born of water and of the Spirit, he cannot enter into the kingdom of God.  That which is born of the flesh is flesh; and that which is born of the Spirit is spirit.  Marvel not that I said unto thee, Ye must be born again.*

Someone has well said that if we are born only once, we die twice, but that if we are born twice, we die only once.  If you have been born physically, but never spiritually in conversion, you will not only die a physical death, but also an everlasting death in hell; but if you have been born both physically and spiritually, you may die a physical death, but you will be translated into eternal life with the Lord.

Let me give you something to think about.  If is far better to speak of eternal life than to speak of everlasting life.  The main idea behind eternal life is not simply that of duration.  It is quite clear that a life that goes on forever could just as easily be in Hell or in Heaven.  You see, the thought of eternal life is the idea of a certain *quality* of life.  What kind?  There is only one person who can properly be described by the adjective eternal, and that one person is God.  Eternal life is the kind of life that God lives; it is God's life.  To enter into eternal life is to enter into possession of that kind of life which is the life of God.  It is to be lifted up above merely human, transient things into the joy and peace that belongs only to God.  Jesus says to have that eternal life "you must be born again."  There is everlasting life in hell, but there is eternal life for the born again child of God.

Jesus did not explain all the mysteries wrapped in the New Birth.  There are some things that we will never understand this side of Heaven; thus, the New Birth can be experienced, but never fully understood. My friend, we don't know how God operates to set the sun and moon and the rain in motion, but we can enjoy what we don't fully understand. Other than God, no one knows exactly how the Holy Ghost brings about the New Birth, but we know that He does it and saves us forever.

### The New Birth IS NOT…

To understand the meaning of the New Birth, we must look at what the New Birth is not.

It is not Reformation. The giving up of some of the wrongs in our lives doesn't mean that we have had a spiritual rebirth, nor does it mean that we have had some great experience with the Lord. Yes, in some cases we reform and clean up our lives externally, but this does not cleanse the heart of its impurities and sin that are displeasing to God. Reformation may help you in this world, but it doesn't bring you eternal life. Reformation is working from the outside to clean up our lives. This work doesn't cleanse the old wicked heart of man.

It is not the environment. All we have to do is look at our government at work to see that putting a person into a better environment with cleaner neighborhoods does not make him a better person. You can take a hog into the house, give him a bath, sprinkle him with the best cologne, and tie your best tie around his neck, but all of that will not change his nature. Let him free and he will run right back to the muck of the pigpen. That is his nature, and the environment of culture doesn't change that nature. My friend, the same is true of the nature of sinful man.

It is not baptism. My friend, you can go to all the different denominational and non-denominational churches in the world and be baptized at all of them. You can even go to the Jordan River and get baptized, but that would not be regeneration; you only got wet.

It is not church membership. Many times I ask a person, "Do you know that you'll go to Heaven when you die?" And they respond "Yes, because I have been a member of such-and-such a church all my life." My friend, Nicodemus held a high position religiously, but Jesus said, *ye must be born again.* Church membership does not mean that one has had an inner change; that he has been born again.

### The New Birth IS…

The New Birth is actually an inner spiritual experience, wrought in the heart by the Holy Ghost. It is not an outer form, but an inner transformation. It is a change from the natural to the spiritual.

All born-again believers have the Holy Spirit. The Bible says that all born-again believers are new creatures: *Therefore if any man be in Christ, he is a new creature: old things are passed away; behold, all things are become new.* (II Corinthians 5:17) This does not occur by the strength or good works of the repenting sinner, but by the Holy Ghost of God. Remember, Jesus said to Nicodemus, *Except a man be born of water and of the Spirit, he cannot enter the kingdom of God.* (John 3:5) Water is the symbol of cleansing. You see, my friend, when Jesus takes possession of our lives, the sins of the past, present, and future are forgiven and forgotten: *That He might sanctify and cleanse it with the washing of water by the word.* (Ephesians 5:26) The Spirit is the symbol of power. When the Holy Ghost takes possession of our lives, it is not only the past that is forgiven and forgotten. Into our lives enters a new power which enables us to be what, by ourselves, we could never be; and to do what, by ourselves, we could never do.

Praise God that every believer receives the Person of the Holy Ghost at the very moment of his transformation. Please do not misunderstand me. When we are converted, we receive all of the Person of the Holy Ghost; but when we are filled with the Holy Ghost, He receives all of us. At the New Birth, He is resident, but when we are filled with the Holy Ghost, He is president. We will talk more about the filling of the Holy Ghost.

In the Old Testament days the Spirit came upon men and then left them. The Spirit came upon prophets to carry out a mission and then departed. But in this day of grace, the Holy Ghost does not come and leave. He abides *unto the day of redemption.* (Ephesians 4:30)

I know there are some sincere people begging God to give them the Holy Ghost. But, my friend, there is no such thing as being saved and NOT possessing the Holy Ghost. Oh, I know some of you have been taught differently; that you are saved and then you get the Holy Ghost at a later date. However, that teaching will not line up with the Word of God. *But ye are not in the flesh, but in the Spirit, if so be that the Spirit of God dwell in you. Now if any man have not the Spirit of Christ, he is none of his.* (Romans 8:9)

That seems to be clear to me! I cannot see how any sincere seeker of truth could misunderstand that plain truth! My friend, bottom line: if you are born of the water and the Spirit, you have the Spirit! If you do not have the Spirit, you are lost! You will have everlasting life in Hell.

## The Necessity of the New Birth

It is necessary because the soul is damned in its original state. God made man in His own image, but that image has been marred by sin and is stumbling along in darkness, desperately needing the New Birth. *And God said, Let us make man in our image, after our likeness: and let them have dominion over the fish of the sea, and over the fowl of the air, and over the cattle, and over all the earth, and over every creeping thing that creepeth upon the earth.* (Genesis 1:26)

*Unto the woman he said, I will greatly multiply thy sorrow and thy conception; in sorrow thou shalt bring forth children; and thy desire shall be to thy husband, and he shall rule over thee. And unto Adam he said, Because thou hast hearkened unto the voice of thy wife, and hast eaten of the tree, of which I commanded thee, saying, Thou shalt not eat of it: cursed is the ground for thy sake; in sorrow shalt thou eat of it all the days of thy life; Thorns also and thistles shall it bring forth to thee; and thou shalt eat the herb of the field; In the sweat of thy face shalt thou eat bread, till thou return unto the ground; for out of it wast thou taken: for dust thou art, and unto dust shalt thou return.* (Genesis 3:16-19)

*Wherefore, as by one man* (Adam) *sin entered into the world, and death by sin; and so death passed upon all men, for that all have sinned.* (Romans 5:12) My friend, if you are coupled to sin, it will take you to hell; If you are coupled to Christ through the New Birth, He will take you to Heaven.

<u>It is necessary because it is the only way of admission to Heaven</u>. The following story is from the late Wilterschel Ford:

A boatman once carried a learned professor across a river on a decrepit ferry. Said the professor to the boatman; "Do you know anything about astronomy?" "No," replied the boatman. "Then one-fourth of your life is gone. Do you know anything about botany?" "No," replied the boatman. "Then another fourth of your life is gone." Just about that time, the boat struck a snag and was going down. "Do you know anything about swimming?" shouted the boatman? "No!" cried the professor. "Then your life is gone," said the boatman.

You may know all about the arts and sciences of this world, but when you face the judgment, all of eternal life will be gone unless you have been "Born again."

Many think that they can seek admittance through the gates of Heaven by doing good works. Heaven's gatekeeper will say, "Have you been born again?" Some will say, "I was a good church member... I was a good husband, father, and neighbor... I was honest... I did good to all men...

I paid my debts."  The gatekeeper says, "Except a man be born again, he cannot enter the Kingdom of God."  That reminds me of the saddest Scriptures in the Bible:  *Not every one that saith unto me, Lord, Lord, shall enter into the kingdom of heaven; but he that doeth the will of my Father which is in heaven.  Many will say to me in that day, Lord, Lord, have we not prophesied in thy name?  and in thy name have cast out devils?  and in thy name done many wonderful works?  And then will I profess unto them, I never knew you: depart from me, ye that work iniquity.*  (Matthew 7:21-23)

### The Method of the New Birth

A man must want to be saved before he can be saved.  A man who is drowning must know it before he calls out for help.  The lost soul must want to be saved before he receives the New Birth.  That want comes from the convicting work of the Holy Ghost and the preaching of God's Word.  The good news is that God never refuses to hear the cry of a lost sinner who seeks to be saved.

<u>The lost soul must surrender fully to God through faith in Christ</u>.  When Christ said that we are to believe in Him, He meant more than an intellectual assent.  The word for "Believe" here is *pisteuo*, which according to the *Strong's Exhaustive Concordance of the Bible*, means "Believe, commit (to trust), put in trust with."  You see, one must trust Him completely, and confess Him publicly.  Men go on in the direction of sin, but when the New Birth comes in, the Holy Ghost comes in, and the life is turned in another direction.

God Himself works the marvelous change. A certain king gave a gold cup to a soldier to show his appreciation of the soldier's good work. "This is too great a gift for me to receive," said the soldier. "But it is not too great a gift for a king to give," replied his sovereign. Although the New Birth and eternal life are great gifts indeed, they are not too great for a loving God to give.

Our Lord had promised His disciples the spiritual vitality they would need to live victorious lives and to render effective service. *But ye shall receive power, after that the Holy Ghost is come upon you: and ye shall be witnesses unto me both in Jerusalem, and in all Judea, and in Samaria, and unto the uttermost part of the earth.* (Acts 1:8)

Paul encouraged the believers in Ephesus to be strong in the power of the Holy Spirit. (Ephesians 5:18) His exhortations about being filled with the Spirit and being strong in the Lord are imperative. Being filled with the Spirit and being strong in the Lord are not optional for believers who want to overcome evil and render service. Again, later in this book we will talk more about the filling. For now we want to get back to the New Birth.

The Father's gift of the Holy Ghost is given when we put faith in Jesus Christ as our Lord and Savior. *That the blessing of Abraham might come on the Gentiles through Jesus Christ; that we might receive the promise of the Spirit through faith.* (Galatians 3:14) The gifts of God are His personal gifts to us. In the Holy Ghost, God gives to us His personal presence.

## The Evidence of the New Birth

Before we move on, I think it is important to look at the evidence of being "Born again."

Christ is nearer. Before the new birth, He seems to be a far-off, vague figure; after the New Birth He becomes our best friend, always by our side, always making His presence known. Before the New Birth, we don't know how to pray properly; after we become born again, we walk and talk with Jesus.

The Bible comes alive. If we are truthful, before the New Birth the Bible was dry, dead, hard to understand. But oh, my friend, after conversion it becomes a living, vital word. You see, Christ becomes alive to you all the way through. A great preacher said that before he was born again he spent his Sunday afternoons reading Nick Carter detective stories, but after he met Jesus he enjoyed those minutes reading His Word.

There is a new attitude toward others. *This is my commandment, that ye love one another, as I have loved you. Greater love hath no man than this, that a man lay down his life for his friends.* (John 15:12-13) That new attitude is one that is produced by the Holy Ghost in the heart of the believer. We cannot be telling racial jokes and be full of the Holy Ghost. We cannot be at odds with other believers and be full of the Holy Ghost. Remember that the manifestation of the Holy Ghost is seen in the fruit of the Spirit: love, joy, peace, longsuffering, gentleness, goodness, faith, meekness, temperance. What we are talking about is agape love (God-like love).

Chapter Three Review

1. There are seven words used in the New Testament in connection with the ministry of the Holy Spirit in this Church age. Give each word and a reference where it can be found:

    a.)_____

    b.)_____

    c.)_____

    d.)_____

    e.)_____

    f.)_____

    g.)_____

2. Explain in your own words what it means to "Be born" and apply it to the second birth._____

_____

_____

_____

_____

_____

3. Explain in your own words the difference between eternal and everlasting. _____

_____

_____

_____

4. **Bonus** Explain the difference between "Death" and "Life," considering that everlasting existence in the lake of fire is called the second "Death" (Revelation 20:14-15) in contrast to eternal "Life" in Heaven. _____

_____

_____

_____

_____

5. The New Birth is NOT:

a.)_____

b.)_____

c.)_____

d.)_____

6. The New Birth IS: _____

_____

7. When the Holy Ghost takes possession of our lives, the past is forgiven and forgotten. Into our lives enters a new power that enables us to:

_____

_____

_____

8. When we are converted,_____;
but when we are filled with the Holy Ghost,

_____.


9. Give the reference that proves that there is no such thing as being saved and not possessing the Holy Ghost:

_____

_____


10. Describe the method of the New Birth:

_____

_____

_____


11. Describe evidence that the New Birth has occurred:

_____

_____

_____

## Chapter 4

# Indwelt By The Spirit

*That good thing which was committed unto thee keep by the Holy Ghost which dwelleth in us.* (II Timothy 1:14)

*But ye are not in the flesh, but in the Spirit, if so be that the Spirit of God dwell in you. Now if any man have not the Spirit of Christ, he is none of his.* (Romans 8:9)

### Born Again Believers Have The Holy Spirit

*Therefore if any man be in Christ, he is a new creature: old things are passed away; behold, all things are become new.* (II Corinthians 5:17) This does not occur by the strength of good works of the repentant sinner, but by the Holy Ghost of God. Let me remind you that every believer receives the Person of the Holy Ghost at the very moment of conversion. Yes, when we are converted we receive all of the Person of the Holy Ghost.

In Scripture you will sometimes see the phrase "Spirit of Christ," as in Romans 8:9. This is the same Holy Ghost that indwells the believers. Jesus departed and is set down at the right hand of the Father, but He promised to send us "another." That other is the Spirit of Christ, Spirit of God, or the Holy Spirit. So we can say that the Holy Spirit dwells within the believer, putting the Spirit of Christ within him.

The power of the Spirit is seen in the word "dwell." The Holy Ghost dwells within the believer: He makes His home, takes up residence and lives within the believer just as we live in our homes.

The power of the Spirit creates the glorious truth of the indwelling presence of the God within the believer and of the believer within God.

The believer is said to be "in the {Holy} Spirit." (Romans 8:9)

The Spirit of God is said to "dwell" in the believer. (Romans 8:9)

The believer is said to have "the Spirit of Christ." (Romans 8:9)Christ is said to be in the believer. (Romans 8:10)

In Clarence Larkin's book <u>Rightly Dividing The Word</u> Chapter 23, "The Reciprocal Indwelling of Christ and the Believer," he points out of the following:

The thoughtful and observing reader of the New Testament will notice a number of paradoxical statements that clearly teach a reciprocal indwelling.

<u>First</u>, of the Father and Jesus: *"I am in the Father and the Father in me."* (John 14:8-11*) "The Father is in me, and I in Him."* (John 10:38) *"That they all may be one, as Thou, Father art in Me, and I in Thee."* (John 17:21)

<u>Secondly</u>, as to Christ and the believer: *"He that eateth My flesh and drinketh My blood, dwelleth in Me, and I in him."* (John 6:56) In the parable of the vine we read, *"Abide in Me, and I in you... He that abideth in Me, and I in him... If ye abide in Me, and My words abide in you..."* (John 15:4,5,7) It is botanically true that the branches abide in the vine, and the vine in the branches. As the two grow, they

grow into each other.  Any attempt to separate them will tear the fibers that interlock with each other and mutilate both.

This "Reciprocal Indwelling" is beautifully illustrated in nature.  Take the four elements, earth, air, water and fire. The plant is in the soil, and the soil is in the plant.  The bird is in the air, and the air is in the bird.  The fish is in the water, and the water is in the fish.  The iron is in the fire, and the fire is in the iron.

The mutual interaction of the plant to the soil, the bird to the air and the fish to the water is necessary to their lives. So the mutual indwelling of Christ and the believer is necessary to the spiritual life of the believer.  When Jesus was about to depart He said, *"Because I live, ye shall live also.  At that day ye shall know that I am in my Father, and ye in me, and I in you."*  (John 14:19-20)

### Born Again Believers Are In Christ

The power of the Spirit **removes** the believer from being "in" the flesh and places him within **Himself**, within Christ.  You see, the power of the Spirit identifies the believer as being "in" Christ.  This is easily seen.  Whatever Spirit dwells within a man, it is that spirit to whom man belongs.

"In Christ" is the position of the believer who has accepted Christ as his personal Savior, has been "born again," regenerated by the Holy Ghost:

"*In Christ justified*"  (Romans 3:24)

"*In Christ sanctified*"  (I Corinthians 1:2)

*"In Christ crucified"* (Galatians 2:20)

*"In Christ ascended"* (Ephesians 1:3)

*"In Christ satisfied"* (Philippians 1:11)

*"In Christ complete"* (Colossians 2:10)

*"In Christ GLORIFIED"* (II Thessalonians 1:10-12)


<u>The believer's position "in Christ" is the same as that of Christ Himself</u>. Believers in Christ are:

<u>Crucified</u> together *"with Him"* (Romans 6:6)

<u>Buried</u> together *"with Him"* (Colossians 2:12)

<u>Quickened</u> together *"with Him"* (Ephesians 2:5)

<u>Risen</u> together *"with Him"* (Colossians 3:1-3)

<u>Heirs</u> together *"with Him"* (Romans 8:17)

<u>Sufferers</u> together *"with Him"* (Romans 8:17)

<u>GLORIFIED</u> together *"with Him"* (Romans 8:17)

This means that when Christ was crucified, I was so identified as a believer in His crucifixion as to be said crucified with Him. You see, when Adam sinned he died to God, and as I am by nature the child of Adam, I died "in Adam" to God. The very moment we accept Christ as our personal savior we are born into the family of the second Adam (Christ), and thus we become partakers of the Christ life; and it follows that whatever was done by Christ was done in and for us, so that when He died on the cross I died with Him; when He was buried I was buried with Him; when He arose from the grave I arose with Him; when He ascended I ascended with Him; when He was glorified I was glorified with Him; and when He shall come again I will come with Him.

## Christ Is In The Born Again Believer

While the new life is conditional on our being "in Christ," the manifestation of that life is dependent on "Christ being in us." The true test of being "in Christ" is fruit bearing. *"Ye shall know them by their fruits."* (Matthew 7:16) *"Wherefore by their fruits ye shall know them."* (Matthew 7:20) My friend, we must distinguish between works and fruits. Works are external, such as service of various kinds, but fruit is internal and is the work of the Holy Ghost in the believer. We will cover this later in this book under "The Fruit of the Spirit," but let me remind you of what I call the saddest verse in the Bible: *Many will say to me in that day, Lord, Lord, have we not prophesied in thy name? and in thy name have cast out devils? and in thy name done many wonderful works? And then will I profess unto them, I never knew you: depart from me, ye that work iniquity.* (Matthew 7:22,23)

You see, my friend, they had works, but Christ was not in them. They were not able to bear fruit. There's a great warning here, especially to those who think you can be saved and yet not be indwelt by the Spirit. You **cannot** trust works of any kind to prove the indwelling of the Spirit of God. The only true and scriptural evidence is in fruit bearing.

A person is spirited, driven to live according to the spirit that is within him. The Holy Ghost has the power to drive the believer to live as Christ lived. We can look at the spirit of a person and test if he has the Spirit of Christ. If he does, then he will bear the fruit of Christ's Spirit. Yes, the Spirit and His fruit are seen in the life of the believer. The true believer proves that he is in Christ by the manifestation of his service, and that Christ is in him by the manifestation of the fruit of the Spirit. This, my friend, shows that the believer is placed and positioned "in Christ" by the life which he lives.

## Indwelt Believers Have Resurrection Power

The Spirit gives life to the spirit of the believer. *And if Christ be in you, the body is dead because of sin; but the Spirit is life because of righteousness. But if the Spirit of Him that raised up Jesus from the dead dwell in you, He that raised up Christ from the dead shall also quicken your mortal bodies by His Spirit that dwelleth in you.* (Romans 8:10-11) Let me make this simple: the body of man does die, but his spirit can live forever if Christ is in him. Note two points:

The Spirit of Christ gives life to the spirit of man, not later but at the very moment a person is converted. Man's body is to die because of sin: remember the body is corrupting, aging, decaying and dying. It is in a process of dying in such a way that it can actually be said to be dead. The body is dying, therefore death is inevitable; however, if in the midst of this death a person accepts Christ, then the Spirit of Christ (the Holy Ghost) enters. When He enters He converts the spirit of man from death to life: *And you hath he quickened who were dead in trespasses and sins; Even when we were dead in sins, hath quickened us together with Christ, (by grace ye are saved;) and hath raised us up together and made us sit together in heavenly places in Christ Jesus.* (Ephesians 2:1,5,6) The word "quicken" means to make alive, to give life, to cause to live, to renew and remake life.

The spirit of man lives because of the righteousness and death of Jesus Christ. *Who his own self bare our sins in his own body on the tree, that we, being dead to sins, should live unto righteousness: by whose stripes ye were healed.* (I Peter 2:24) *For he hath made him to be sin for us, who knew no sin; that we might be made the righteousness of God in him.* (II Corinthians 5:21)

The spirit of man lives by living a righteous and godly life. *There is therefore now no condemnation to them which are in Christ Jesus, who walk not after the flesh, but after the Spirit.* (Romans 8:1)

The Spirit quickens the mortal body in the future, in the great day of redemption.

So also is the resurrection of the dead. *It is sown in corruption; it is raised in incorruption: It is sown in dishonor; it is raised in glory: it is sown in weakness; it is raised in power: It is sown a natural body; it is raised a spiritual body. There is a natural body, and there is a spiritual body.* (I Corinthians 15:42-44)

*Now this I say, brethren, that flesh and blood cannot inherit the kingdom of God; neither doth corruption inherit incorruption. Behold, I show you a mystery; We shall not all sleep, but we shall all be changed, In a moment, in the twinkling of an eye, at the last trump: for the trumpet shall sound, and the dead shall be raised incorruptible, and we shall be changed. For this corruptible must put on incorruption, and this mortal must put on immortality. (I Corinthians 15:50-53)*

Please note, the mortal body shall be quickened and made alive: The mortal body is the same body that died. The person is the very same person. The mortal body is given a totally new life; its elements are recreated and remade into a prefect and eternal body. The new body is to be given the power and energy of the eternal elements, eternal molecules, eternal atoms. All will be arranged so that the mortal body becomes an immortal body.

### Two great assurances of the believer's resurrection

Jesus' resurrection assures the believer that he, too, shall be raised from the dead. The resurrection of Christ proves that God is, that He does exist and that He cares. There is no power on earth that can raise a man from the dead. Only a supreme, eternal, powerful God can do that. Only God can give life to dead matter and to the dust of the earth. The very fact that Jesus Christ was raised from the dead proves that God exists and that He cares.

The resurrection also proves that Jesus Christ is who He claimed to be, the Son of God Himself. It proves that Christ was sent to earth to reveal the ideal righteousness for man and to die and to arise from the dead for man. *And what is the exceeding greatness of his power to us-ward who believe, according to the working of his mighty power, Which he wrought in Christ when he raised him from the dead, and set him at his own right hand in the heavenly places. (Ephesians 1:19-20)*

*And declared to be the Son of God with power, according to the spirit of holiness, by the resurrection from the dead. (Romans 1:4)*

The resurrection of Christ proves that Jesus Christ is the Savior of the world. It proves that Christ is the very one whom God sent to earth to save men from death and to give life.

*For God so loved the world, that he gave his only begotten Son, that whosoever believeth in him should not perish, but have everlasting life. (John 3:16)*

*By which also ye are saved, If ye keep in memory what I preached unto you, unless ye have believed in vain. For I delivered unto you first of all that which I also received, how that Christ died for our sins according to the scriptures. And that he was buried, and that he rose again the third day according to the scriptures. (I Corinthians 15:2-4)*

The resurrection of Christ proves that He is "the Spirit of life" and that He can give the same "Spirit of life" to men. He can raise men from the dead, even as He rose from the dead.

*But if the Spirit of him that raised up Jesus from the dead dwell in you, he that raised up Christ from the dead shall also quicken your mortal bodies by his Spirit that dwelleth in you. (Romans 8:11)*

For if we believe that Jesus died and rose again, even so them also which sleep in Jesus will God bring with him. (IThessalonians 4:14)

*Blessed be the God and Father of our Lord Jesus Christ, which according to his abundant mercy hath begotten us again unto a lively hope by the resurrection of Jesus Christ from the dead, To an inheritance incorruptible, and undefiled, and that fadeth not away, reserved in heaven for you. (I Peter 1:3,4)*

The assurance of the Holy Ghost, of Him who indwells the believer, assures the believer that he, too, shall be raised from the deed. The very same Spirit who raised up Christ shall raise up the believer – He is the power and energy of life, and He indwells every believer; therefore, He shall raise up the believer. And declared to be the Son of God with power, according to the spirit of holiness, by the resurrection from the dead. (Romans 1:4)

*Knowing that he which raised up the Lord Jesus shall raise up us also by Jesus, and shall present us with you.* (II Corinthians 4:14)

## Indwelt Believers Have Adoption Power

*But as many as received him, to them gave he power to become the sons of God, even to them that believe on his name.* (John 1:12)

*For ye have not received the spirit of bondage again to fear;*
*but ye have received the Spirit of adoption, whereby we cry,*
*Abba, Father.* (Romans 8:15)

My friend, we have a new position as born-again children of God, and with that new position comes a great number of blessings, some of which are absolute transformations. We have the assurance of our sonship because we have been indwelled with the Holy Ghost.  The whole sphere of our lives has been changed.  We once lived completely centered on self and self's desires, but now we are centered on the Lord Jesus Christ.  It is true that the two centers fight against each other... the flesh lusting against the Spirit, and the Spirit against the flesh.  The reality of our new centering on Christ is an assured fact.  It is adoption that allows us to have <u>full</u> assurance of faith.

Romans 8:15 begins with the word "for."  This word is a hinge that ties the whole passage together.  We have been brought out of death and into life.  We have been established in Christ as a new priest, around which all life is to revolve.  When God raised Our Lord from the dead, He raised us up together with Him.  Read Ephesians, chapter two, to get a better understanding.  You see, the victory is assured, because *as many as received Him, to them gave He power to become the sons of God; because we have not received the Spirit of bondage again to fear.*  (John 1:12, Romans 8:15)

<u>Adoption...  The Spirit adopts the believer.</u>  Note two very significant points:

<u>The Spirit delivers man from a terrible spirit... the spirit of bondage</u>.  Now, make close note of what the bondage is:  It is <u>fear</u>.  Man is gripped by the bondage of fear, usually expressing some anxiety, dread, alarm, danger, apprehension, and even terror.  Man is usually feeling some enslavement, some subjection to some form of fear.  Everyone is familiar with the spirit of fear.  We are enslaved and held captive by it.  What causes fear:  Anything and everything can arouse fear.  A few of the more prominent

things are: suffering, Failure, Unemployment, Punishment, Condemnation, Disease, Loss of Spouse, Death.

The point is that the Holy Ghost delivers the believer from the bondage of fear. How? By adoption. Don't miss this...by <u>actually</u> adopting the believer as a Son of God.

*But when the fulness of the time was come, God sent forth His Son, made of a woman, made under the law, To redeem them that were under the law, that <u>we</u> might receive the adoption of sons. And because ye are sons, God hath sent forth the Spirit of his Son into your hearts, crying, Abba Father. (Galatians 4:4-6)*

<u>The Spirit gives access into God's presence.</u> The access to God is because the believer has been adopted as a Son of God. Remember, the Spirit is called the "Spirit of adoption." Adoption is such a significant work of the Holy Ghost that it is called the "Spirit of adoption." As we stated earlier, the believer actually receives the Spirit of adoption. And the sense, the consciousness, the awareness, the knowledge that he is a Son of God. Oh yes, the born-again believer is a Son of God with <u>all</u> the privileges of sonship, including the privilege of entering into God's presence anytime and anyplace. It's this privilege that enables the believer to break the bondage of fear and to conquer the spirit of fear. Always keep in mind that no matter what the believer faces, he is able: To enter the presence of God, To lay his fear before God, To cry out, "Father, Father!" and To know that God will help him, for God loves him as His adopted son.

*I am the door: by me if any man enter in, he shall be saved, and shall go in and out, and find pasture. (John 10:9)*

Therefore being justified by faith, we have peace with God through our Lord Jesus Christ: By whom also we have access by faith into this grace wherein we stand, and rejoice in hope of the glory of God. (Romans 5:1,2)

For through him we both have access by one Spirit unto the Father. (Ephesians 2:18)

I think we can safely say that every true believer knows what it is to fear in this life, and he knows what it is to experience God delivering him from the fear. He should know what it is to be a true Son of God, a son whom God loves so much that He will move the world in order to meet the need of His dear child. God's love for His adopted son is as great as God's sovereign power.

## Adoption

Another power of the Spirit is the power to bear witness with our spirit. He bears witness to four glorious truths:

The Holy Ghost bears witness that we are the sons of God.

Very simply stated, the Holy Ghost quickens our hearts with the perfect knowledge and the complete confidence that we are "sons of God." Look how clearly Scripture proclaims this glorious truth, the truth which, as believers, we want the world to know. You see, the Spirit sheds abroad the love of God in our hearts. He spreads the knowledge that God loves us and spreads it all through our being. *And hope maketh not ashamed; because the love of God is shed abroad in our hearts by the Holy Ghost which is given unto us.* (Romans 5:5)

The Holy Ghost bears witness that we are the heirs of God.

If God is <u>truly</u> our Father, then we inherit what He possesses:

<u>We are heirs of eternal life...</u>

*That being justified by his grace, we should be made heirs according to the hope of eternal life. (Titus 3:7)*

<u>We are heirs of salvation...</u>

*Are they not all ministering spirits, sent forth to minister for them who shall be heirs of salvation?* (Hebrews 1:14)

<u>We are heirs of the promises made to Abraham...</u>

that is, the promises to inherit the world and to become the citizens of a great nation of people. The heirs of God shall inherit a great kingdom, that is, the new heaven and earth. *For the promise, that he should be the heir of the world,was not to Abraham, or to his seed, through the law, butthrough the righteousness of faith.* (Romans 4:13)

*And if ye be Christ's, then are ye Abraham's seed, and heirs according to the promise.* (Galatians 3:29)

*That the Gentiles should be fellowheirs, and of the same body, and partakers of his promise in Christ by the gospel.* (Ephesians 3:6)

We are heirs of glory... *And if children, then heirs; heirs of God, and joint-heirs with Christ; if so be that we suffer with him, that we may be also glorified together.* (Romans 8:17)

*The eyes of your understanding being enlightened; that ye may know what is the hope of his calling and what the riches of the glory of his inheritance in the saints.* (Ephesians 1:18)

*Giving thanks unto the Father, which hath made us meet to be partakers of the inheritance of the saints in light.* (Colossians 1:12)

We are heirs of righteousness…

*By faith Noah, being warned of God of things not seen as yet, moved with fear, prepared an ark to the saving of his house; by the which he condemned the world, and became heir of the righteousness which is by faith. (Hebrews 11:7)*

We are heirs of the grace of life…

*Likewise, ye husbands, dwell with them according to knowledge, giving honour unto the wife, as unto the weaker vessel, and as being heirs together of the grace of life; thatyour prayers be not hindered. (I Peter 3:7)*

*The point I'm trying to make is that the Holy Ghost is the One who seals the truth in our hearts. He is the earnest [guarantee] of our inheritance. (Ephesians 1:14)*

There is much more that we inherit as sons of God, but this study will be limited to the Holy Ghost.

## Indwelt Believers are Fellow-Heirs with Christ

The Holy Ghost bears witness that we are joint-heirs with Christ. This is an astounding truth and promise. We shall inherit <u>all</u> that God has and all that Christ is and has. We will be given the privilege of sharing in all things with the Son of God, Himself. <u>However</u>, to be a joint-heir with Christ does not mean that believers will receive an equal amount of the inheritance with Christ. Rather, it means that believers are fellow heirs with Christ; that is, believers will <u>share</u> in the inheritance of Christ.  In other words, we will share Christ's inheritance with Him.   Remember, the believer is the bridegroom of Christ; therefore, we share with Him.

Being a fellow-heir with Christ means at least three glorious things: It means that we share in the nature, position, and responsibility of Christ.

<u>Fellow Heirs by Nature</u>:  Christ is the Son of God, the very being and energy of life and perfection; therefore, we share in the inheritance of His nature.  We receive:

- The adoption as a son of God (Galatians 4:4-7, I John 3:1)
- The sinless nature of being blameless (Philippians 2:15)
- Eternal life (John 1:4, 3:16, 10:10, 17:2,3; I Timothy 6:19)
- An enduring substance (Hebrews 10:34)
- A glorious body (Philippians 3:21; I Corinthians 15:42-44)
- Eternal glory and honor and peace (Romans 2:10)
- Eternal rest  (Hebrews 4:9; Revelation 14:13)
- An incorruptible body (I Corinthians 9:25)
- A righteous being (II Timothy 4:8)

<u>Fellow Heirs by Position:</u>  Christ is the exalted Lord, the sovereign Majesty of the universe, the Lord of Lords and King of Kings; therefore; we share in the inheritance of His position.  We receive:

- The position of exalted beings (Revelation 7:9-12)
- A citizenship in the Kingdom of God (James 2:5; Matthew 25:34)
- Enormous treasures in Heaven (Matthew 19:21; Luke 12:33)
- Unsearchable riches (Ephesians 3:8)
- The right to surround the throne of God (Revelation 7:13-17, 20:4)
- The position of a King (Revelation 1:6, 5:10)
- The position of a priest (Revelation 1:6, 5:10, 20:6)
- The position of glory (I Peter 5:4)

Fellow Heirs by Responsibility:  Christ is the Sovereign Majesty of the Universe, the One who is ordained to rule and oversee all; therefore, we share in the inheritance of His responsibility.  We receive:

- The rulership over many things (Matthew 25:23)
- The right to rule and hold authority (Luke 12:42-44, 22:28-29) Eternal responsibility and joy (Matthew 25:21-23)
- Rule and authority over cities (Luke 19:17-19)
- Thrones and the privilege of reigning forever

### The Holy Ghost Bears Witness That We Are Conquerors Over Suffering

These passages will give some idea of what Scripture teaches when it speaks of the believer being a co-heir with Christ:

*Blessed are ye, when men shall revile you, and persecute you, and shall say all manner of evil against you falsely, for my sake.* (Matthew 5:11)

*And ye shall be hated of all men for my name's sake: but he that endureth to the end shall be saved.* (Matthew 10:22)

*As it is written, For thy sake we are killed all the day long; we are accounted as sheep for the slaughter. Nay, in all these things we are more than conquerors through him that loved us.* (Romans 8:36,37)

*If we suffer, we shall also reign with him: if we deny him, he also will deny us.* (II Timothy 2:12)

*Yet if any man suffer as a Christian, let him not be ashamed; but let him glorify God on this behalf.* (I Peter 4:16)

*But the God of all grace, who hath called us unto his eternal glory by Christ Jesus, after that ye have suffered a while, make you perfect, stablish, strengthen, settle you.* (I Peter 5:10)

## You Cannot Be A Believer And Not Be Indwelt By The Holy Ghost

There are many today who teach that a person can be born again and yet not have the Holy Ghost. This teaching is not of the Bible. This teaching is in error. My friend, without the Holy Ghost we are powerless. If the believer needs anything, and he does, he needs the power of God's Spirit. Let me just close on the indwelling by pointing out from Romans chapter eight what the power of the Holy Ghost is. Take your Bible and follow along:

1.) The Spirit gives life. (Romans 8:2-4)

2.) The Spirit pulls the mind to spiritual things.

3.) The Spirit dwells within the believer. (Romans 8:9)

4.) The Spirit gives life to the spirit of the believer. (Romans 8:10-11)

5.) The Spirit gives the power to mortify, put to death, our evil deeds (Romans 8:11-12)

6.) The Spirit leads the believer, identifying him as a Son of God. (Romans 8:14)

7.) The Spirit adopts (Romans 8:15)

8.) The Spirit bears witness with our spirit. (Romans 8:16-17)


*I am come that they might have life, and that they might have it more abundantly.* (John 10:10)


Chapter 4 Review (Read Romans 8 with this section)

1. All things do not become new by _____, but by _____.


2. What is the "Spirit of Christ?"_____


3. What does the word "dwell" mean?_____


4. What is "The Reciprocal Indwelling of Christ and the Believer?"

_____

_____

_____

_____

5.  Give your own example of reciprocal dwelling in nature. _____

_____

6.  The position "In Christ" of the believer who has accepted Christ as his personal savior is (give references):

_____

_____

_____

_____

_____

_____

_____

_____

7.  The new life is conditioned on being _____ _____, but the manifestation of that life is dependent on _____.

8. The true test of being "in Christ" is _____ _____.

9.  What is the difference between works and fruits?

_____

_____

_____

10.    What is the saddest verse in the Bible?

_____

_____

_____

11.    A person is drive to live by _____

_____.

12.  The spirit of man lives because of _____

_____ and by living _____.

13.    The Holy Spirit quickens the believer's
_____ at conversion and his
_____ at the day of redemption.

14.    What are two assurances of the believer's
resurrection?    _____

_____

_____

15.    What two centers fight against each other?

_____

_____

_____

16. It is _____ that allows us to have full assurance of faith.

17. Christ is a new _____ around which all life is to revolve.

18. What are the two significant points every believer should understand about adoption?_____
_____
_____

19. Another power of the Spirit is the power to _____.

20. The Spirit bears witness to what four glorious truths?

a)_____
b)_____
c)_____
d)_____

21. List the things we inherit as sons of God:

a)_____
b)_____
c)_____
d)_____
e)_____
f)_____

22. The word "earnest" means: _____

_____

23.  Being a fellow-heir with Christ means at least three glorious things.  List each with verse reference.

a)_____

b)_____

c)_____

24.  List the manifestations of the Holy Ghost's power given in Romans 8, with verse reference.

a)_____

b)_____

c)_____

d)_____

e)_____

f)_____

g)_____

h)_____

*Chapter 5*

# Sealed and Anointed by the Spirit

*And grieve not the Holy Spirit of God, whereby ye are sealed unto the day of redemption.* (Ephesians 4:30)

### God has sealed us with the Holy Spirit.

God is the identifying seal upon our heart until the day of redemption. To understand this better is to know the difference between reformation and regeneration. In Matthew 12:43-45, we have the story of an unclean spirit that leaves a man, goes out and walks through dry places seeking rest, finds no rest – then returns to the man out of which he came. He finds his house empty, swept, and garnished, but there is **no one** inside, and there is **no seal** on the door. This is a picture of reformation, not regeneration. When the devil goes out at the command of God, the Holy Ghost comes in, and He not only comes in, but He seals the heart with Himself. When the demons come to the door of the heart of a believer, he finds the seal of God on the door.

Today, some wear signet rings as jewelry, but in the ancient world the ring bearing the insignia of an official was a form of power, authority, or validation. When stamped into hot wax, the ring transferred a seal or insignia. If a letter or a public proclamation bore the seal of a king or a governor, that was proof that it was genuine. And so it is with the believer; the seal is our guarantee. God *seals* believers. The word means to mark, to stamp, to place a seal upon. God places His seal, His stamp, His mark upon believers.

*Who hath also sealed us, and given the earnest of the Spirit in our hearts.* (II Corinthians 1:22) The word "earnest" is very important in understanding the sealing of the Holy Ghost. "Earnest" means pledge, guarantee, a down payment, deposit, security and payment. The Holy Spirit is given to the believer to give the believer perfect assurance of his salvation. We know that we are redeemed, that we are God's cherished possession by the Holy Spirit who seals us. The Holy Spirit was the first installment paid on us to guarantee that the rest would be paid. He is the engagement ring that guarantees the marriage. God has given the Holy Ghost as the guarantee of eternal life. He is the down payment, the advanced payment on God's promise to believers.

*Jude, the servant of Jesus Christ, and brother of James, to them that are sanctified by God the Father, and preserved in Jesus Christ, and called:* (Jude 1) Here we see the word "preserved" means to be kept, to be guarded and watched over. The believer is a person who is:

- Watched over by God
- Guided and directed by God day by day
- Strengthened by God to walk through all the trials and temptations of life
- Protected from all the enemies of life, even death

- To be escorted into Heaven quicker than the blink of an eye when the time comes for him to leave this world
- Given life, both abundant and eternal
- Given assurance of God's presence and love through all of life

Yes, my friend, the true believer is a person who is sealed and preserved by God. He is a person who is looked after and cared for by God. The believer is a person who has placed his life into Jesus Christ; he is a person who is trusting Jesus Christ to save him. It is only the true believer in Jesus Christ whom the Holy Spirit seals and preserves.

## The Holy Spirit Guides Sealed Believers

*I have yet many things to say unto you, but ye cannot bear them now. Howbeit when he, the Spirit of truth, is come, he will guide you into all truth: for he shall not speak of himself; but whatsoever he shall hear, that shall he speak: and he will shew you things to come. He shall glorify me: for he shall receive of mine, and shall shew it unto you.* (John 16L12-14)

Let's look at three things that the Holy Spirit guides believers through.

The Holy Spirit guides by always speaking the truth. Christ said that He had many things to say to the apostles, but they were not able to "bear" (handle, grasp) them yet. This is not an opening for "impartations" or the words "the spirit told me." The Spirit will never go against Christ. Christ tells the Spirit what to say and how to guide believers. Let us remember that when Christ said, "I have yet many things to say unto you, but ye cannot bear them now," the death, burial and resurrection had not yet taken place. They would only be able to bear that truth after the fact.

The Holy Spirit guides by leading into all truth. That's why the Holy Spirit is called "The Spirit of Truth." He speaks only the truth and guides into "all the truth." The truth, of course, is Jesus Christ Himself. The Spirit leads the believer to Christ, the Truth, and teaches him all the truth about Christ. *Jesus saith unto him, I am the way, the truth, and the life: no man cometh unto the Father, but by me.* (John 14:6) There is a difference between telling someone the truth and living the truth before them. The one who lives the truth literally becomes the truth.

What we must understand is that Jesus Christ is the embodiment of truth. He is the picture of truth. God not only talks to man about Himself, God shows man what He is like in the person of Jesus Christ. Man can look at Jesus Christ and see the truth of God.

*But when the Comforter is come, whom I will send unto you from the Father, even the Spirit of truth, which proceedeth from the Father, he shall testify of me:* (John 15:26)

*We are of God: he that knoweth God heareth us; he that is not of God heareth not us. Hereby know we the spirit of truth, and the spirit of error.* (I John 4:6)

The Holy Spirit guides by showing, announcing and declaring things to come. After Jesus arose, the Holy Spirit was the one who led the apostles to write the New

Testament and to foresee the things revealed in its pages. Since that day, the Holy Spirit is the One who takes the things revealed in the Word and shows, declares and announces them to the heart of the sealed believer.

*But as it is written, Eye hath not seen, nor ear heard, neither have entered into the heart of man, the things which God hath prepared for them that love him.  But God hath revealed them unto us by his Spirit:  for the Spirit searcheth all things, yea, the deep things of God.  Now we have received, not the spirit of the world, but the spirit which is of God; that we might know the things that are freely given to us of God.*  (I Corinthians 2:9-10, 12)

### The Holy Spirit Comforts And Helps Sealed Believers

In the thirteenth chapter of John's gospel, Jesus told His disciples of His coming betrayal and death.  They were very saddened by this news, and in John 14:1 He said to them, *"Let not your hearts be troubled, ye believe in God, believe also in me."*  Then we notice in verse 16 of the same chapter He promised, *"And I will pray the Father, and he shall give you another Comforter, that he may abide with you for ever."*  John 14:16

This promise was fulfilled on the day of Pentecost. The Holy Spirit came, inaugurating the dispensation of Grace, in what is called the Church Age.  The Holy Spirit is still a resident on earth today, and will be here to comfort and help believers until the Church is raptured up to meet Jesus in the clouds in the air.

Four times Jesus referred to the Holy Spirit as "the Comforter." John 14:16 is the first time; the second reference is in John 14:26; the third reference is in John 15:26, but the fourth time must have been the most shocking to the disciples. *"Nevertheless I tell you the truth; It is expedient for you that I go away: for if I go not away, the Comforter will not come unto you; but if I depart, I will send him unto you."* (John 16:7) They had given up everything to follow Christ only to hear Him say, "It is expedient for you that I go away." What a shock. Then notice verse 12, *"I have yet many things to say unto you, but ye cannot bear them now."*

Yes, my friend, there were many things the disciples did not understand as Jesus talked with them for three and one-half years during His public ministry. Many things He would have said to them, but because of their dullness and unbelief He did not say to them. But thank God for the seal of the Holy Ghost in the presence of Jesus at the door of your heart.

### On What Ground Is The Believer Sealed?

*Labour not for the meat which perisheth, but for that meat which endureth unto everlasting life, which the Son of man shall give unto you: for him hath God the Father sealed.* (John 6:27)

The Lord Jesus Christ was sealed on the ground of His own divine, personal perfection: but with the believer it is different. The Holy Ghost is not given to believers because of anything we possess within ourselves: we are not sealed because of our righteousness, sanctity, worship or devotion to God. Believers are sealed with the Holy Spirit solely because we have been redeemed with the precious blood of the Lord Jesus Christ.

*This is the covenant that I will make with them after those days, saith the Lord, I will put my laws into their hearts, and in their minds will I write them; And their sins and iniquities will I remember no more. Now where remission of these is, there is no more offering for sin. Having therefore, brethren, boldness to enter into the holiest by the blood of Jesus.* (Hebrews 10:16-19)

*And almost all things are by the law purged with blood; and without shedding of blood is no remission.* (Hebrews 9:22)

See, my friend, we are not sealed because of what we are or because of what we have accomplished, but because we stand in the finished work and perfect sacrifice offered by Jesus once and for all, never to be repeated.

It is at the very moment we put faith in the finished work of Jesus that we are born of the Spirit and sealed with the Spirit. Let me make one thing very clear: I have Scripture to prove that the believer is sealed at conversion, rather than at some subsequent period in his life. The Bible tells us exactly when the believer receives the Holy Ghost, and when he is sealed with the Spirit. Please get your King James Bible and follow along.

In Romans chapters 3 and 4, we find the unfolding of the way of justification and salvation for ungodly sinners who should spend eternity in hell; and then in Romans 5:1

we read, *"Therefore being justified by faith, we have peace with God through our Lord Jesus Christ."* Then in verse 5 of chapter 5 we read, *"And hope maketh not ashamed; because the love of God is shed abroad in our hearts by the Holy Ghost which is given unto us."* It seems to me that even a young Christian could see that, according to the Word of God, justification by faith is accompanied instantaneously by the gift of the Holy Ghost. The sad part is that there are those who oppose this, yet there is no Scripture that even suggests that a believer is saved apart from the Holy Ghost coming into the heart and sealing it. Watch, my friend: When the unbeliever hears the Gospel and believes on the Lord Jesus Christ, receiving His finished work and shed blood by faith, that very moment he is indwelt and sealed by the Holy Ghost.

The Holy Ghost can only apply this seal upon the heart and mind of that person who is born again. I think most people have forgotten that we do not become a Christian because we receive Him; we become a Christian because He receives us. The Word never suggests that you can receive Him by your acts alone, but rather that you surrender to Him, totally trusting Him to take complete charge of your life. It is a life and death commitment of the past, present and future that He then receives from you and gives you the power to become His child. For a clear description of this fact we just need to look at John 1:12: *"But as many as received him, to them gave he power to become the sons of God, even to them that believe on his name."* My friend, no one is saved by the single act of the individual receiving Jesus Christ. The Holy Ghost must act as the Savior's "vicar" or agent to work a divine miracle of redemption.  He calls this being "born again."

*Jesus answered and said unto him, Verily, verily, I say unto thee, Except a man be born again, he cannot see the kingdom of God.  Nicodemus saith unto him, How can a man be born when he is old?  Can he enter the second time into his mother's womb, and be born?  Jesus answered, Verily, verily, I say unto thee, Except a man be **born** of **water** and of the **Spirit**, he cannot enter into the kingdom of God.*  (John 3:3-5)

The plan of salvation is clearly stated.  We hear the Word, we believe the Word, we receive the Word, and the Holy Ghost performs the miracle of regeneration in our hearts.  He then takes up His abode in the heart, and He is the seal.

### How Long Is The Believer Sealed?

*In whom ye also trusted, after that ye heard the word of truth, the gospel of your salvation:  in whom also after that ye believed, ye were sealed with that Holy Spirit of promise.*  (Ephesians 1:13)  *And grieve not the Holy Spirit of God, whereby ye are sealed unto the day of redemption.*  (Ephesians 4:30)

Look closely at Ephesians 4:30, where Paul says we are sealed unto the day of redemption.  We must admit that this verse does not refer to the redemption of the soul, because the soul is redeemed when the sinner believes and receives the Gospel.  The day of redemption for the soul has already come for every born again child of God, but there is a day of redemption in the future.

*And not only they, but ourselves also, which have the first-fruits of the Spirit, even we ourselves groan within ourselves, waiting for the adoption, to wit, the redemption of our body. For we are saved by hope: but hope that is seen is not hope: for what a man seeth, why doth he yet hope for?* (Romans 8:23,24)

These bodies in which we live are not yet redeemed, but they will be redeemed when Jesus appears, for we shall then be like Him.

*Beloved, now are we the sons of God, and it doth not yet appear what we shall be: but we know that, when he shall appear, we shall be like him; for we shall see him as he is.* (I John 3:2)

You see, my friend, our bodies belong to Christ; they are the temple of the Holy Ghost:

*What? Know ye not that your body is the temple of the Holy Ghost which is in you, which ye have of God, and ye are not your own? For ye are bought with a price: therefore glorify God in your body, and in your spirit, which are God's.* (I Corinthians 6:19,20)

If Jesus tarried long enough, this tabernacle of flesh will die, decay and return to dust. There is a day coming when these corruptible bodies will put on incorruption. The living saints at Christ's coming will be changed:

*Behold, I shew you a mystery; We shall not all sleep, but we shall all be changed, In a moment, in the twinkling of an eye, at the last trump: for the trumpet shall sound, and the dead shall be raised incorruptible, and we shall be changed.* (I Corinthians 15:51,52)

Yes, my friend, we will be given a body like Jesus' glorious resurrection body. This is the redemption for which every born again child of God is waiting in anxious anticipation and, yes, it could be at any moment. No man knows the day or the hour when Jesus will come in Rapture, but it could be today. But we are sealed until "the day of redemption."

### The Seal Is A Matchless Act

The Holy Spirit actually puts the identification of Jesus upon your conscience and will. The message to the Hebrews describes this clearly.

*For this is the covenant that I will make with the house of Israel after those days, saith the Lord; I will put my laws into their mind, and write them in their hearts: and I will be to them a God, and they shall be to me a people: And they shall not teach every man his neighbor, and every man his brother, saying, know the Lord: For all shall know me, from the least to the greatest.* (Hebrews 8:10,11)

Don't miss this: the seal of the Holy Ghost inscribes the laws of God upon our minds and hearts. A godly life is the joy of every believer sealed with the Holy Ghost.

The minister won't have to badger the true believers with the commandments of God. The seal on the heart will reflect the nature of the lord Jesus Christ and sin will become repulsive. When we understand the sealing, we will understand why the early church turned the world upside down. Souls that are wrought upon by the Holy Ghost in this kind of redemption become saints of God, reflecting the life of Jesus Christ. *"And hath raised us up together, and made us sit together in heavenly places in Christ Jesus."* (Ephesians 2:6) This is not religion, but total transformation.

## Anointed By The Spirit

*The Spirit of the Lord is upon me, because he hath anointed me to preach the gospel to the poor; he hath sent me to heal the brokenhearted, to preach deliverance to the captives, and recovering of sight to the blind, to set at liberty them that are bruised, to preach the acceptable year of the Lord.* (Luke 4:18,19)

Webster's 1828 American Dictionary of the English Language defines "anointed" as *"The Messiah or Son of God, consecrated to the great office of Redeemed;* **call the Lord's anointed.***"*

We know that there is only one Redeemer, the Lord Jesus Christ, but I believe we can safely say that every believer has been anointed with the Holy Ghost in order to consecrate him to perform his calling. Again, turning to Webster's 1828 American Dictionary, we read "Consecrate": *To canonize; to exalt to the rank of a saint; to enroll among the gods; To set apart and bless the elements in the Eucharist.*

You say, Brother Mike, how does this relate to me? I'm glad you asked. All believers have been exalted to the rank of saints.

*Paul, called to be an apostle of Jesus Christ through the will of God, and Sosthenes our brother, unto the church of God which is at Corinth, to them that are sanctified in Christ Jesus, called to be saints, with all that in every place call upon the name of Jesus Christ our Lord, both their's and our's.* (I Corinthians 1:1,2)

*Paul, an apostle of Jesus Christ by the will of God, and Timothy our brother, unto the church of God which is at Corinth, with all the saints which are in all Achaia.* (II Corinthians 1:1)

*Paul, an apostle of Jesus Christ by the will of God, to the saints which are at Ephesus, and to the faithful in Christ Jesus.* (Ephesians 1:1)

I think you get the picture. We were once sinners on our way to Hell, but now we are saints on our way to Heaven because of the work of our Redeemer, the Lord Jesus Christ.

Believers have been enrolled by God in the Lamb's Book of Life, written in by the blood of the Lamb.

The anointing comes at the time of conversion and is the work of the Holy Ghost. This anointing renders us holy, and separated to God.

*But ye have an unction (anointing) from the Holy one, and ye know all things... But the anointing which ye have received of him abideth in you, and ye need not that any man teach you: but as the same anointing teacheth you of all things, and is truth, and is no lie, and even as it hath taught you, ye shall abide in him.* (I John 2:20,27)

I like the way these verses are explained in the Liberty Annotated Study Bible: *"This unction then, predisposes John's readers to recognize and respond to*

*God's truth, but not to arrive at it independently of the Biblical and apostolic word. Had the readers been capable of knowing all things apart from written and spoken instruction, I John would not need to have been written."* (p.1964)

The same would hold true that if we were capable of knowing all things apart from written and spoken instruction we wouldn't have needed Paul, Peter, Luke, James, Mark, Matthew, Jude, or John. We could take out *"And he gave some, prophets; and some, evangelists; and some, pastors and teachers; for the perfecting of the saints, for the work of the ministry, for the edifying of the body of Christ."* (Ephesians 4:11,12) The key is that the evangelists, the pastors, and teachers must be anointed by the Holy Ghost. We should be well aware of the godhood and holiness of our Savior Jesus Christ, but the Christ of flesh and blood had a profound ministry to fulfill. He had to be about His *"Father's business."* (Luke 2:49) Only as flesh and blood could he accomplish his present task as described in Luke 4:18. Remember, He said, *"The Spirit of the Lord is upon me, because He hath anointed me to preach the Gospel."* As Jesus preached the Gospel, it had not found its completion until the death, burial, and resurrection of Jesus Christ.

### Preaching Of The Gospel

Anointed with the Spirit, Jesus preached Good News that the Kingdom of God was at hand. He proclaimed a message of forgiveness, a message of repentance, a message of peace to the guilt-ridden and anguished of the world. Let us never forget He preached an uncompromising truth: *"Verily, verily, I say unto thee, except a man be born again, he cannot see the kingdom of God. Marvel not that I said unto thee, Ye must be born again."* (John 3:3,7) An anointed preacher would never water down what Jesus himself preached. You see, Jesus Christ knew there was no way to Heaven but by Him.

"To The Poor" – Here, Jesus is speaking of the spiritual bankruptcy that is found in every heart outside of Jesus Christ. Let's say it this way: The Good News, when received by the spiritually bankrupt, extends to them wealth in Christ Jesus. We see an example of this in Revelation 2:9, when Jesus was speaking to the church at Smyrna:

*I know thy works, and tribulation, and poverty, (but thou art rich) and I know the blasphemy of them which say they are Jews, and are not, but are the synagogue of Satan.* (Revelation 2:9)

The Roman government had taken all they had, yet God said, "you are rich." Oh, my friend, the day will come when all we have is what we laid up in Heaven. What does your Heavenly account look like?

"Heal The Broken-Hearted" – Do you realize how much we are loved? You see, God refused to view mankind only from His heavenly throne, but He literally took upon Himself flesh and blood. In this way He was able to personally understand what was required in the healing process. Though Christ never sinned, He knew what our needs were.

*Wherefore in all things it behoved him to be made like unto his brethren, that he might be a merciful and faithful high priest in things pertaining to God, to make reconciliation for the sins of the people. For in that he himself hath suffered being tempted, he is able to succor them that are tempted.* (Hebrews 2:17,18)

Yes, my friend, God does give the needed help and comfort to a person's broken heart. Through the compassion of Christ, the repentance of the sinner, the aid of the Holy Spirit, and the preaching, teaching, or counseling of an anointed man of God, the person can find his ruptured heart mended.

"Preach Deliverance To The Captives" – The sad thing about this verse is that some teach that this deliverance is only an earthly deliverance – deliverance from oppression caused by other people. The deliverance performed by Christ is two-fold: First, spiritual release and second, physical release. The important thing to remember is that it's only available to individuals who recognize their enslavement and are willing to repent and accept the freedom found in Christ.

*Then said Jesus to those Jews which believed on him, if ye continue in my word, then are ye my disciples indeed; and ye shall know the truth, and the truth shall make you free. They answered him, we be Abraham's seed, and were never in bondage to any man: how sayest thou, Ye shall be made free? Jesus answered them, Verily, verily, I say unto you, Whosoever committeth sin is the servant of sin. And the servant abideth not in the house for ever: but the Son abideth ever. If the Son therefore shall make you free, ye shall be free indeed.* (John 8:31-36)

You see, we are prisoners of our own lusts and ungodly sins. Christ has offered each prisoner of Satan an opportunity to be set free. This is spiritual deliverance. Don't miss this: the physical deliverance is a by-product of the spiritual. When we yield to the righteous life of Christ, our old habits of sin (drinking, drugs, smoking, perversion, etc...) are crushed and we receive newness of life in Christ.

*For we are unto God a sweet savour of Christ, in them that are saved, and in them that perish.* (II Corinthians 2:15)

"Recovering Of Sight To The Blind" – No matter what the so-called faith healers tell us, every physically blind person who has accepts Jesus Christ as Savior will not automatically have his sight restored. The concept involved is spiritual sight, and the reason for this is found in II Corinthians 4:3,4:

*But if our gospel be hid, it is hid to them that are lost: In whom the god of this world hath blinded the minds of them which believe not, lest the light of the glorious gospel of Christ, who is the image of God, should shine unto them.*

When individuals let Jesus Christ into their hearts, they receive Spiritual "20/20" vision. As they grow, they receive new insights, and their eyes are opened to a brand new vision. That vision is to do the will of God.

"To Set At Liberty Them That Are Bruised" – The Good News is that Jesus desires that people everywhere be freed from the consequences of sin.

*The Lord knoweth how to deliver the godly out of temptations, and to reserve the unjust unto the day of judgment to be punished.* (II Peter 2:9)

Sin degrades the body and leaves it scarred and mangled. In my work at Good Samaritan Ministries, I see the scars that alcohol, drugs, and illicit sex leave.  Go to a hospital and see the results of sin on bodies and minds.  Go to families where sin runs rampant and see the bruises it leaves on spouses and children.  Jesus came to restore the bruised to a place of wholeness and happiness.

Preach The Acceptable Year Of The Lord

*For after that in the wisdom of God the world by wisdom knew not God, it pleased God by the foolishness of preaching to save them that believe.*  (I Corinthians 1:21)

It is interesting to me that so many people confess to be Christian but don't like preaching.  Yet, Jesus Himself established this method for proclaiming the truth to reach the multitudes.  Our Lord believes in the value of preaching.  Do you?

The phrase "acceptable year of the Lord" indicates that the time of God's truth has now appeared.  It is now the proper time to yield to the revelation of the Father.

*For even hereunto were ye called:  because Christ also suffered for us, leaving us an example, that ye should follow his steps.*  (I Peter 2:21)

My friend, to follow the steps of Jesus we must have the anointing of the Holy Spirit.


Chapter Five Review

1.  How does the sealing of the Holy Spirit make a difference between reformation and regeneration?

_____

_____

_____

_____

2. What does the word "seal" mean?

_____

_____

_____

3. A seal on an object proves that the object is

_____.

4. "Earnest" means:

_____

_____

_____

5. The Holy Spirit was the first _____
to guarantee _____

6. "Preserved" means:

_____

_____

_____

7. List the seven things done for the believer by the sealing of the Holy Spirit:

   a._____

   b._____

c._____

d._____

e._____

f._____

g._____


8. List the three things the Holy Spirit guides the believer through:

a._____
_____
_____

b._____
_____
_____

c._____
_____
_____

## Chapter 6

# Filled With The Spirit

*"And be not drunk with wine, wherein is excess; but be filled with the Spirit."* (Ephesians 5:18)

We fundamental believers seem to want to skip this verse, but we cannot. Who was the author of these words? Was it Paul? If you answer yes, you are incorrect. The Holy Ghost of God wrote them. We must remember that these words are not of human but of divine origin. Paul was only God's messenger boy and we must never forget that we, too, are just messenger boys.

With that in mind, we must give attention to this command; *"Be filled with the Spirit"* for it comes from the very breath of Almighty God! We have no right to say it's too controversial, for this is a command just as *"ye must be born again,"* thus, we must look at this command as we would any other command of God. The Spirit-filled life is the plan of God for all born-again believers. It is only when we live under the control of the Holy Ghost that we can labor in God's power.

There are seventeen verses before we get into the command to *"be filled with the Spirit."* Let's look at them briefly. They reveal what must take place before the filling.

Ephesians 5:1 says, "Be ye therefore followers of God, as dear children." The idea here is to be imitators of God. The Greek word "followers" is "mimetai" and means "imitator".

Christ said: *Be ye therefore perfect, even as your Father which is in heaven is perfect.* (Ephesians 5:48)

God demanded: *Ye shall be holy: for I the Lord your God am holy.* (Leviticus 19:2)

Paul declared: *For whom he did foreknow, he also did predestinate to be conformed to the image of his Son, that he might be the firstborn among many brethren.* (Romans 8:29)

Peter charged: *But as he which hath called you is holy, so be ye holy in all manner of conversation; Because it is written, Be ye holy; for I am holy.* (I Peter 1:15,16)


Ephesians 5:2 says, *"And walk in love, as Christ also hath loved us, and hath given himself for us an offering and a sacrifice to God for a sweetsmelling savour."* This is sacrificial love (agape).

Christ said: *But I say unto you, Love your enemies, bless them that curse you, do good to them that hate you, and pray for them which despitefully use you, and persecute you.* (Matthew 5:44)

Christ also said: *By this shall all men know that ye are my disciples, if ye have love one to another.* (John 13:35)

Peter declared: *Seeing ye have purified your souls in obeying the truth through the Spirit unto unfeigned love of the brethren, see that ye love one another with a pure heart fervently.* (I Peter 1:22)

John charged: *Beloved, let us love one another: for love is of God; and every one that loveth is born of God, and knoweth God. He that loveth not knoweth not God; for God is love.* (I John 4:7,8)


Ephesians 5:3 says, *"But fornication, and all uncleanness, or covetousness, let it not be once named among you, as becometh saints."* One <u>has</u> to keep his body free of all fornication; he <u>has</u> to keep his body free of all uncleanness.

*Now the works of the flesh are manifest, which are these; adultery, fornication, uncleanness, lasciviousness...* (Galatians 5:19a)

One has to keep his body free of covetousness. *And he said unto them, Take heed, and beware of covetousness: for a man's life consisteth not in the abundance of the things which he possesseth.* (Luke 12:15)

Notice the verse in Ephesians says, *"Let it not be once named"* – not even mentioned once, my friend. Not only are we not to engage in these sins, but we are not even to talk about them. Not name, talk about, or mention in our conversation.


Ephesians 5:4 says, *"Neither filthiness, nor foolish talking, nor jesting, which are not convenient: but rather giving of thanks."*

"Filthiness" – He is never, not once, to be engaged in "filthiness" – using the mouth in obscene, shameful, foul, polluted, base, or immoral conduct and conversation. What an indictment for our day... a day of sodomy and perversion. And note, the word refers to both conduct and speech. How polluted and foul-mouthed so many have become... so much so that society could easily be known as a second Sodom and Gomorrah." (from the <u>Preacher's Outline and Sermon Bible, Galatians, Ephesians, Philippians, and Colossians</u>, Volume 9, Page 198.)

*Wherefore lay apart all filthiness and superfluity of naughtiness, and receive with meekness the engrafted word, which is able to save your souls.* (James 1:21)

"Foolish Talking" – The idea is talk that has no purpose to it. I believe we could add sinful, foolish, silly and corrupt talk.

Job was asked: *Should a wise man utter vain knowledge, and fill his belly with the east wind? Should he reason with unprofitable talk? Or with speeches wherewith he can do no good?* (Job 15:2,3)

Solomon declared: *A fool uttereth all his mind: but a wise man keepeth it in till afterwards.* (Proverbs 29:11)

Ecclesiastes 10:13 states: *The beginning of the words of his mouth is foolishness: and the end of his talk is mischievous madness.*

"Jesting" – Telling off-colored jokes, being cunning, talking foolishly, poking fun, making wise cracks, and using these things to attract attention and win favors.

Paul said:  *For of this sort are they which creep into houses, and lead captive silly women laden with sins, led away with divers lusts.*  (II Timothy 3:6)

Peter declared:  *For he that will love life, and see good days, let him refrain his tongue from evil, and his lips that they speak no guile.*  (I Peter 3:10)

"Not Convenient" – inappropriate, unsuitable, unfitting; talk that is not becoming to a follower of Christ.

Paul said:  *And whatsoever ye do in word or deed, do all in the name of the Lord Jesus, giving thanks to God and the Father by him.*  (Colossians 3:17)

Solomon declared:  *The words of a wise man's mouth are gracious; but the lips of a fool will swallow up himself.*  (Ecclesiastes 10:12)


Ephesians 5:5,6 says, *"For this ye know, that no whore-monger, nor unclean person, nor covetous man, who is an idolater, hath any inheritance in the kingdom of Christ and of God.  Let no man deceive you with vain words:  for because of these things cometh the wrath of God upon the children of disobedience."*  I have put both of these verses together because God is giving a solemn warning.  There three significant points in these two verses:

"Uncleanness" – Uncleanness has no part with God.  Please notice the specific sins mentioned in these verses that doom a person:

1.)  Whoremonger – one who engages in illicit sexual intercourse, fornication, or prostitution:  immoral behavior

2.)  Unclean person – one with dirty thoughts or behavior

3.) Covetous – strongly wanting what belongs to another

4.) Idolater – one who worships or places something or someone as God, or gives that object or person m ore devotion than he does God.

## "Deceivers With Their Words"

There are people who might tell us:

- That sex is a normal and natural thing:
- That a one-time affair will not hurt anyone.
- That prostitution is acceptable & will not harm us.
- That homosexual behavior is normal.
- That securing possessions is normal behavior.

   "Storing up" is acceptable.

   "Storing up" builds position.

   "Storing up" or securing possessions helps your ego and self-image.

Paul, however, warns us: *But evil men and seducers shall wax worse and worse, deceiving, and being deceived.* (II Timothy 3:13)

John said: *For many deceivers are entered into the world, who confess not that Jesus Christ is come in the flesh. This is a deceiver and an antichrist.* (II John 1:7)

## Two Main Deceptions About Christianity

William Barclay points out in The Letters To The Galatians And Ephesians (p.192) that there were and still are two main deceptions about Christianity:

There were those Christians who felt that they could say and do anything and still be acceptable to God. This argument came primarily from those outside the Church who held the same argument. This idea finds its roots in the philosophy of Gnosticism. Gnosticism said that man is both body and spirit. They felt that the spirit is the only part that really concerns God. What a man does with his body does not matter: the body is not important. It makes no difference whatsoever if a man abuses his body: gorges, dirties, and fouls it.

However, Christianity counters, "Never!" Both body and soul are important. We see this in Jesus Christ. He honored the body by taking a body upon Himself. (Hebrews 2:14) Today, He honors the body by making it the "Holy Temple" for His presence in the person of the Holy Spirit. (I Corinthians 6:19) Jesus Christ is interested in the body of man as well as the spirit of man. He is interested in the whole man, and He saves the whole man.

There were those, primarily within the church, who felt that sin was irrelevant. How much a person sinned just did not matter. God is love and He forgives and forgives, no matter how much wrong we do. In fact, some argued that the more we sin, the more God is able to forgive and demonstrate His mercy in us. So why not live the way we want? Why not sin and let God's mercy and love show through us, for the more we sin, the more God's grace will be seen. But Christianity counters, "Never!" God's love and grace are not only a give and a privilege, but also a responsibility and an obligation.

However, God says because of these things the wrath of God comes upon the children of disobedience. (Ephesians 2:2, 5:6) The wrath of God is a decisive anger, a deliberate anger that arises from His very nature of holiness. It is an anger that is righteous, just, and good... that stands against the sins and evil of man... their dirt and pollution and immoralities... their injustices and neglects in a world that reels under the weight of the lost, starving, diseased, and dying masses. God could never overlook the whoremonger who destroys family life nor the contentious man who overlooks the needy. He would not be God: He would not be loving or just if He overlooked such evil people.

Paul reminds us: *For the wrath of God is revealed from heaven against all ungodliness and unrighteousness of men, who hold the truth in unrighteousness.* (Romans 1:18)

*For this ye know, that no whoremonger, nor unclean person, nor covetous man, who is an idolater, hath any inheritance in the kingdom of Christ and of God. Let no man deceive you with vain words: for because of these things cometh the wrath of God upon the children of disobedience.* (Ephesians 5:5,6)

Before we go on and you think I am talking about Lordship salvation, or that a man can lose his salvation, let's look at I Corinthians 6:9-11):

*Know ye not that the unrighteous shall not inherit the kingdom of God? Be not deceived: neither fornicators, nor idolaters, nor adulterers, nor effeminate, nor abusers of themselves with mankind, nor thieves, nor covetous, nor drunkards, nor revilers, nor extortioners, shall inherit the kingdom of God. And such were some of you: but ye are washed, but ye are sanctified, but ye are justified in the name of the Lord Jesus, and by the Spirit of our God.*

Paul goes on in verse twelve to remind us that we are saved only by the work of Jesus Christ. Watch:

*All things are lawful unto me, but all things are not expedient: all things are lawful for me, but I will not be brought under the power of any.*

I felt I had to remind readers that we are talking about being "filled by the Holy Spirit," not about salvation that is by grace through faith plus anything. Anyway, this oasis was free, and I hope refreshing.

Ephesians 5:7 says, *Be not ye therefore partakers with them.* To be a follower of Jesus Christ, we must separate ourselves from the unclean. In other words, we are not to take part in the sins discussed, but we are also to separate ourselves from those who do take part, even if they are Christians.

Paul commands us: *Now we command you, brethren, in the name of our Lord Jesus Christ, that ye withdraw yourselves from every brother that walketh disorderly, and not after the tradition which he received of us.* (II Thessalonians 3:6)

In Ephesians 5:8, Paul uses those words, *"For ye were."* He is now going to show us the evidence of one who is filled with the Spirit. Now the writer finds himself in a transformation period. We will now go to verse eighteen and work our way backwards:

*And be not drunk with wine, wherein is excess; but be filled with the Spirit.*

Being a former drunk and drug addict who now directs a substance abuse program, I feel I need to deal with the first part of this verse. At first glance, you could get the picture that drinking is O.K. The meaning of excess is excessive behavior. We are to walk carefully and strictly by not becoming drunk with alcohol. You see, drunkenness is a work of the flesh and it often leads to other sins of the flesh.

In Ephesus there was a religious group known as the cult of Dionysus who believed that deliverance or salvation was to found through use of alcohol. They hoped to escape depression, disappointments, grief, and their failure through drunkenness. They believed that salvation came through escape flight. The sad thing is that they have too many descendants today.

Yes, my friend, the Spirit-filled life is the plan of God for each of His children. We must live under the control of the Holy Ghost. Verse ten states, *"Proving what is acceptable unto the Lord."* We have already covered in the book the facts that:

Every believer has received the gift of the Holy Spirit.

The Holy Spirit has baptized every believer into the body of Christ.

Every believer has been sealed by the Holy Ghost.

Now, every believer is commanded to be filled with the Holy Spirit.

This filling is not just for a select few and it is not a one-time event. This command is in the present tense which means that the believer is to be constantly filled with the Spirit; he is to keep on being filled. Let me say it this way; the Holy Spirit wants to fill the believer continuously. The reason for this is that the filling is the personal manifestation of Christ to the believer who walks obediently day by day. It makes us aware of His presence, of His leadership – moment by moment.

Ephesians 5:17 says, *"Wherefore be ye not unwise, but understanding what the will of the Lord is."*

How do we know that will? "Be filled with the Spirit." This consciousness is the believer's privilege, but the responsibility rests upon each of us individually.

Jesus said: *"He that hath my commandments, and keepeth them, he it is that loveth me: and he that loveth me shall be loved of my Father, and I will love him, and will manifest myself to him. Judas saith unto him, not Iscariot, Lord, how is it that thou wilt manifest thyself unto us, and not unto the world?"* (John 14:21,22)

Dear reader, please take not that this special manifestation is only in the believer. It is not seeing a physical manifestation as some claim. The sad thing is that most who claim to have seen a physical manifestation claim to be Spirit-filled Christians. We can see by the Word of God that this is not the way God manifests Himself to us. He dwells within us and manifests Himself to us through His Word and His Spirit.

The problem with most of us is that we are so full of darkness that we look for God in all the wrong places. We look for outward signs and wonders instead of that which is inward. The special manifestation of Christ only happens when there is a deep consciousness of love between the Lord and us. (Re-read John 14:21,22) My friend, if you miss this, you will never experience the manifestation that is given only to the believer who wants two things:

He receives the commandments of Christ. To have the commandments of Christ means that the believer has searched the Word of God, he has it hidden in his heart, and applies it. David said, *"Thy word have I hid in mine heart, that I might not sin against thee."* (Psalm 119:11)

He keeps the commandments of Jesus. James writes: *"But be ye doers of the word, and not hearers only, deceiving your own selves."* (James 1:22)

As I look at Judas's question, *"How is it that thou wilt manifest thyself unto us, and not unto the world,"* I cannot help but believe that Judas was thinking like most so-called Spirit-filled Christians – in terms of a physical manifestation, a visible appearance. Today, we have what is called the "Toronto Blessing" and the "Pensacola Revival." Both depend on physical manifestation: shaking, jerking, laughing, or crying uncontrollably. Some people bark like dogs, roar like lions, crow like roosters, or moo like cows.

Oral Roberts "saw" the manifestation of a 900-foot Jesus. The sad thing is not one of the manifestations are based upon the Word of God: *"And not unto the whole world?"*

The term "manifestation" indicates Jesus' disclosure of His person, His nature, His goodness.  May I say it this way:  He illuminates Himself within our hearts and lives.

One of the saddest things in Christianity is settling for a substitute when we can have the real thing.  In conclusion, I must share with you what I feel are a couple of the saddest verses in the Bible:

*Not everyone that saith unto me, Lord, Lord, shall enter into the kingdom of Heaven; but he that doeth the will of my Father which is in Heaven.  Many will say to me in that day, Lord, Lord, have we not prophesied in thy name?  and in thy name have cast out devils?  and in thy name done many wonderful works?  And then will I profess unto them, I never knew you:  depart from me, ye that work iniquity.  Therefore whosoever heareth these sayings of mine, and doeth them, I will liken him unto a wise man, which built his house upon a rock.*  (Matthew 7:21-24)

Chapter Six Review

1. The Spirit Filled life is the plan of _____ for all born again _____.

2. But as He which hath called you is _____, so be ye _____ in all manner of _____; Because it is written, Be ye _____ for I am Holy.  (I Peter 1:15-16)

3. One has to keep his body free of all
_____; he has to keep his body free of all
_____.

4. List the specific sins listed in Ephesians 5:5,6 that doom a person:

     a._____

     b._____

     c._____

     d._____

5. God's love and grace are not only a _____ and a privilege, but also a _____ and an obligation.

6. The Spirit filled _____ is the plan of God for each of His _____.

# A Note From The Author

Dear Reader, do you know for sure if you were to die today that you would go to Heaven, or do you have some doubt?

The road to Heaven is clearly laid out in the Bible in the book of Romans. If you carefully study the verses and do what the Bible says, you can be certain that Heaven will be your home when you die!

Please study the following four steps:

1. **Admit that you are a sinner.**

   Romans 3:10 *"As it is written, There is none righteous, no, not one."*

   Romans 3:23 *"For all have sinned, and come short of the glory of God."*

2. **Realize that a price must be paid for your sin.**

   Romans 5:12 *"Wherefore, as by one man sin entered into the world, and death by sin; and so death passed upon all men, for that all have sinned."*

   Romans 6:23 *"For the wages of sin is death; but the gift of God is eternal life through Jesus Christ our Lord."*

3. **Believe that Jesus loves you and paid the price for your sin when He died on the cross.**

   Romans 5:8 *But God commendeth his love toward us, in that, while we were yet sinners, Christ died for us.*

4. **Call on Jesus and ask Him to save you, and receive His payment for your sins.**

   Romans 10:9,10 *That if thou shalt confess with thy mouth the Lord Jesus, and shalt believe in thine heart that God hath raised him from the dead, thou shalt be saved. For with the heart man believeth unto righteousness; and with the mouth confession is made unto salvation.*

   Will you call on Jesus today?

   Admit you are a sinner.

   Admit that your sin will send you to Hell.

Believe that Jesus loves you and paid the price for your sin.

Call or write us and ask us for Discipleship Course #1. There is no charge.

**Pastor Mike McClary**

Good Samaritan Ministries

2307 Hull Street

Richmond, VA  23224

Or Call:  1-804-231-9995


You can also learn more about Pastor McClary's Ministries at:


www.ccb-church.com

.

## Books by Dr. Michael D. McClary

|  | Price | Qty |
|---|---|---|
| What about me?  The Holy Spirit | $9.95 | _____ |
| The Church – Then and Now | $7.00 | _____ |
| Biblical Tongues | $7.00 | _____ |
| Biblical Marriage | $7.00 | _____ |
| Have We Forgotten Who We Are? | $4.00 | _____ |

Subtotal     _____

Please add 5% Sales Tax     _____

Total     _____

### Shipping and Handling

$2.00 for the first book

$1.00 for each additional book ordered.

Please mail order form and check or money order to:

Good Samaritan Ministry

2307 Hull Street

Richmond, Virginia  23224

Made in the USA
Columbia, SC
21 December 2019

85661971R10067